Gang Member

Gang Member

Another Side of Democracy

P.J. Brown

New York

This story is true. Some of the names have been substituted because I forgot them.

—P.J. Brown

Vantage Press and the Vantage Press colophon
are registered trademarks of Vantage Press, Inc.

Cover design by Susan Thomas

FIRST EDITION

Published by Vantage Press, Inc.
419 Park Ave. South, New York, NY 10016

Manufactured in the United States of America
ISBN: 978-0-533-16240-6

Library of Congress Catalog Card No: 2009904251

0 9 8 7 6 5 4 3 2 1

To Mary

In Memory of Grand Master Sang Kuy Shim

and Vanessa Nathan

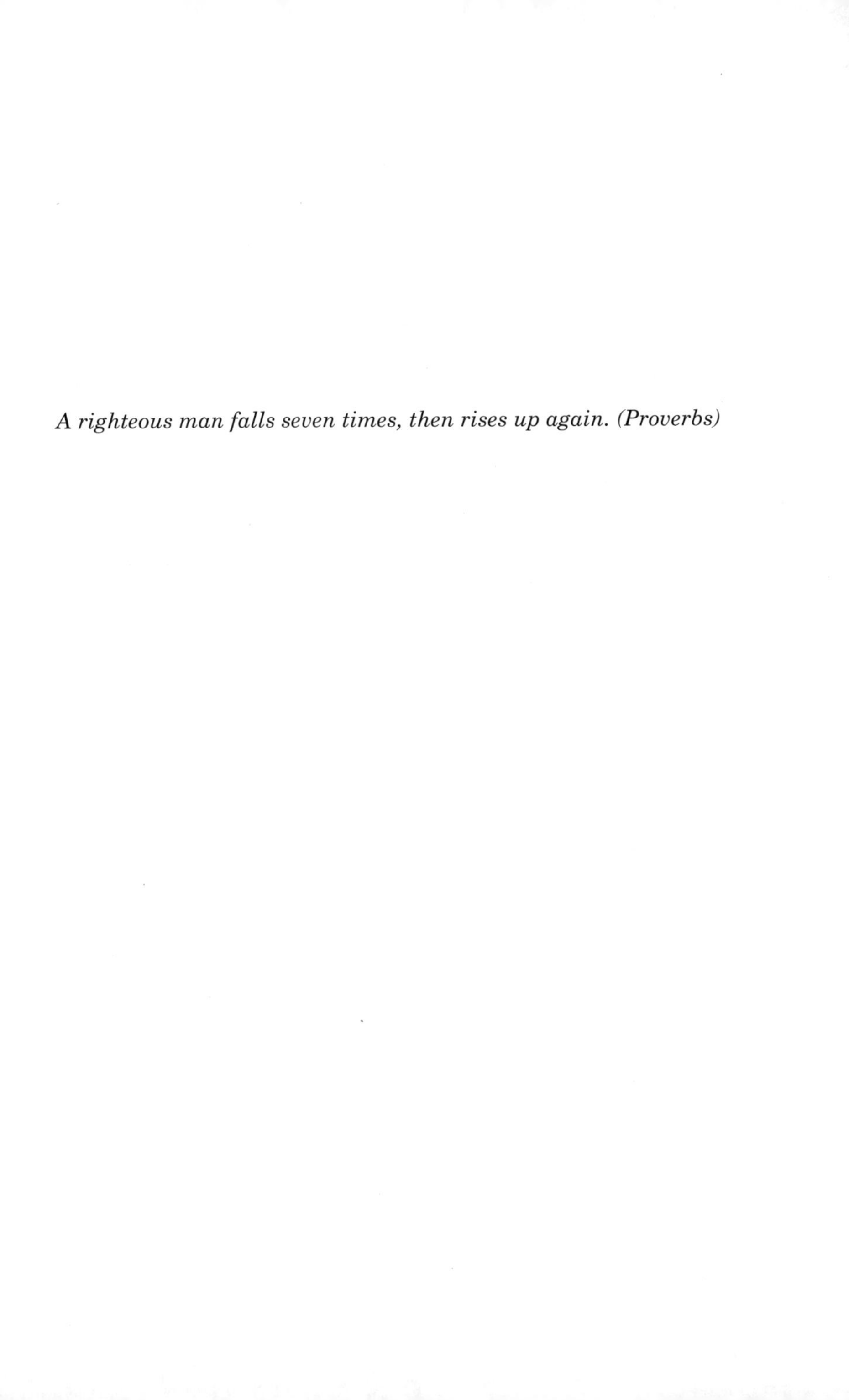

A righteous man falls seven times, then rises up again. (Proverbs)

Contents

Foreword

I lost my job in 1977 after I was incarcerated for not paying child support. After having worked seven years for the Chrysler corporation in Detroit, Michigan, and five years for the Federal Government before that, I found myself homeless. I lived in a park in Los Angeles until I was rescued by a gang that controlled an area of Los Angeles called "the Jungle." I became a gang member and eventually came to be third in command.

When I moved back to my place of birth, Montgomery, Alabama, I joined the Dexter Avenue King Memorial Baptist Church. While relating a gang experience in Sunday School, one of the Church's Deacons became interested in my story. "We can't help a lot of our young men today because we don't know the mindset. You have really given us an idea of the mindset of some of these gang members."

From that statement, I was inspired to write the entire story of my gang experience. The story is true.

—P. J. Brown

Gang Member

One
The Time Is At hand

"The time is at hand!" Kojac said, as he entered Omar's apartment. The apartment was located in an area of Los Angeles known as The Jungle. It was a high crime area. The name "The Jungle" was a good indication of what the place was like. Omar lived in an apartment building in the La Brea Avenue, Coliseum Boulevard area. The entrance to his apartment was at the top of two flights of stairs.

There was a balcony overlooking a swimming pool that had been cemented over. The apartment owner had the pool covered after a child had drowned in it. Omar's door was never locked, and most of the time the apartment was filled with people. The music was always loud like there was a party. On this particular day, a group of men sat in the living room, waiting for Kojac.

Omar had a huge fish tank. He liked to raise predatory fish. The men loved to watch the feedings. Some of the men would stare at the tank as if it was a movie.

Hearing the door open, Johnnie-Reb reached for his pistol. Seeing it was Kojac, he pulled his shirt back down. "It's about time you got here, man."

"You'rc late as usual, Kojac," Omar said. "These brothers were about to leave."

"I'm here now, that's all that counts. I was with a

young lady. If you had seen how fine she was, you'd 'understand.' "

"This is business, Kojac. Let's get our business taken care of before all that other bullshit," Omar said angrily. Omar had two distinct personalities. He was a kind-hearted person who would fall for any sad story. Children loved him and he always took time to play with them. Anyone could go to Omar for help and a lot of people did. He was able to help because he was a fairly big-time drug dealer and known to be a cold-blooded killer. Omar was known as the "Godfather" in the Jungle. Omar, Kojac, and the other members of the gang had met in San Quentin prison. All of them were ex-cons except for Johnnie-Reb.

Kojac ignored Omar and walked towards the kitchen. "Where's Evelyn?" he asked. Evelyn was coming from the kitchen as Kojac was entering. The two met and hugged. The voices of several other females could be heard in the back. All of the women knew to stay out of the living room when Omar was conducting business. "We got business to take care of, Kojac!" Omar yelled.

"You're just jealous, Omar," Evelyn said, smiling and squeezing Kojac tighter.

"I'm not jealous, Marie," Omar said in a childlike tone. 'Business is business."

Omar called her Marie; everyone else called her Evelyn. They had both come from Beaumont, Texas. Evelyn had always looked out for Omar, even during the years he spent in San Quentin. She liked to flirt with other men in front of Omar, as if she was trying to make him jealous. That might explain why Omar would sometimes strike her unexpectedly and without an explanation. He was always sorry later and would comfort her with some kind of expensive gift. The beatings and the gifts came pretty often; she had an impressive collection of jewelry.

Kojac was from Mississippi. He was already strong and muscular before going to prison. Serving time in San Quentin had given him a body that would have qualified him for Mr. Universe. He was popular with women because of his build. Women would whistle at him when they passed him on the street. Kojac considered himself a professional robber, bragging that he came from a long line of robbers. Those who knew him never trusted him alone with a woman because he was also a known rapist. There were stories about women he had raped on his short stays out of prison and stories about men that he had raped while in prison.

"I had better let you go, Evelyn," Kojac said, removing his hands from Evelyn's waist. 'Your old man is getting angry."

"We'll talk later," Evelyn replied, as she turned toward the kitchen.

Kojac turned to Omar. "You're too serious, man. You need to relax more."

"Forget the dumb shit, Kojac," Omar replied. "Kool came up short again."

"He's not holding out on us," Johnnie-Reb interrupted. "He just keeps letting them bitches get dope from him on credit. Or for free. Either way, that's why he's always coming up short."

"How the other guys doing?" Kojac asked.

"Everyone else is fine; we got good workers, except Kool," Johnnie-Reb answered.

"What do you want to do, Omar?" Kojac asked.

"It ain't that much money. Just don't give the fool any more dope to sell," Omar answered.

"I say we kill him!" Kojac replied nonchalantly. Johnnie-Reb could not hide his anxiety. He stood up. "Wait Kojac, it's not worth that. He's just weak for bitches, he don't mean nothing. I agree with Omar, let's just don't give him any more dope to sell."

Johnnie-Reb was the only native Californian in the group. He was also the only one who had not served time in San Quentin. He had been in jail a lot, but he had managed to avoid prison. He did work out a lot and had muscles comparable to the ex-cons.

"His weakness is his own problem," Kojac replied. "We have to set an example if we are going to run a successful business. We should be a lot bigger than we are now. We just waste too much time playing these small-time games. The time is at hand, men. We need to look into the new drugs. We need new organization. We need to get our share of the money that is being passed on them streets. If we don't get it, there are some guys out there who will.

"As for Kool, we have put three contracts on that nigger already. Three times we said we were going to kill him, three times we called it off. No fool should be that lucky. I want Kool beat to death and I want everyone to know it was us who did it. I want the body to be left in the streets so that the word will spread around the Jungle. The pushers will think twice before crossing us and the dope-heads will know we mean business."

Omar rubbed his head. "Kool is one lucky muther-fucker. We can't keep letting him get by. He's history. Now, what kind of new drugs are we talking about?"

"They are going wild over this new stuff called angel dust. The people who know how to make the stuff are making money like a muther. We need to get in on it."

"We've been hearing about the stuff on the news. A

lot of people are tripping out, going crazy, and dying off of that stuff. It may not be a good business to go into."

"There ain't no other way. It's the drug of choice on the streets now." Kojac's expression suddenly changed as he looked at his watch. "I got to go, you guys. Let's go ahead and split the money."

Omar left the room and returned with a briefcase filled with money. He tossed stacks of bills to each of the men. Kojac put his share away and headed for the door. "Omar, tell Evelyn and the girls bye for me. I'm going to meet some people who can get us started in the angel dust business." He turned to Johnnie-Reb. "Get a couple of guys and take care of Kool," he said as he walked out of the door. He paused before he let the door close.

"You guys tell everybody you see. You have seen the Divine One and the time is at hand."

Kool was busy going about his morning chores when he glanced over his shoulder to notice it was almost daybreak. Like a vampire, he had to be finished before the sun rose. As he glanced over his shoulder, he saw the security guard creeping upon him, gun drawn and pointed at his head. The guard was in the process of yelling "Freeze!" when Kool turned on one knee and executed a karate sweep. The guard was knocked from his feet, his gun flying from his hand. Kool dropped the packages of bread and rolls he was accumulating. He quickly ran for the hole he had cut in the fence at the back of the supermarket. Once he got outside, he grabbed a box of bakery products he had placed there earlier and ran for the Jungle.

Kool lived on Coliseum Street, around the corner from Omar. He was a veteran of the United States Army. He was attending school on the GI bill; however, the educational assistance check was not enough for him to live on. Kool supported himself by pushing drugs, stealing, and doing odd jobs for the local gang leaders.

He had a fairly large number of single parents who came to him to purchase fresh bread at discounted prices. The bakery trucks delivered the baked goods to the market before dawn. The deliveryman would place the baked goods inside a fenced-off area in back of the market. Kool would wait for delivery, crawl in through a hole he had cut in the fence, and have fresh bread for sale before the market opened.

He had not stolen as much bread as he had wanted to that night. However, when he got the boxes inside his apartment, he was pleased with what he had. Customers were at the door as soon as it was daylight. The women, most of them wearing robes or nightclothes, would negotiate with Kool, trying to get the most bread for the least amount of money. Kool always tried to talk the women into sexual arrangements. The ones who flirted with him could talk him out of anything.

Lately he had been keeping special packages for Harriet. She lived in the same apartment building as he. He was infatuated with her and she had been getting a lot of free drugs and bread. There were other women, but Harriet was Kool's dream girl. She was light-skinned, and had long hair and a dynamite body. He stood daydreaming about Harriet when the realization that the enforcers would be coming after him made him look out of his window.

His timing was right. He was about to turn away from the window when he saw Johnnie-Reb and two other men coming through the alley across the street. Kool waited until the three men had begun climbing the stairs to his apartment before he threw down a rope and climbed from his front window to the ground beneath. When he touched the ground, he began running as fast as he could. He could hear the men breaking down his door as he made his escape.

Kool ran as fast as he could and as far as he could. He was exhausted and drenched with sweat when he reached the Adams Motel. He waited and watched carefully to make sure he had not been followed, then he rented a room, found his way to the bed, and passed out.

Kool slept the entire day and night. It was early the next day when he and I met in the courtyard. I was doing my morning exercises; he was checking the streets to see if Johnnie-Reb and the boys were on his trail. When he was satisfied that the streets were empty, he came over to speak.

"What kind of exercise do you call that?"

"This is called a form," I said. "It's martial arts. The Japanese word is kata; the Korean word is *hyung*."

"I do a little kung fu myself," Kool said as he threw some kicks and punches.

"What type?"

"I don't have a style; I do a little of it all."

"I practice Tae Kwon Do," I said. "My teacher is grand master Sang Kyu Shim in Detroit."

"It looks like you know what you're doing. Maybe you can teach me some."

"Sure, I'm in room 208. Come up anytime."

"You get high?"

"No, I try to keep my focus on martial arts. I know a couple of ladies who are looking for some weed, though."

"I got just what they are looking for. If you know anybody looking for weed or cocaine, I'm your man. I'll drop by a little later."

Kool came to the room to visit later that day. He met

my wife Mary and our friend Mary Underwood. Kool set out a few joints to be sociable. When he found out the ladies liked cocaine, he began to pull out his stash. As usual, Mary Underwood had made him pull out much more than he had intended. He was angry with himself for getting into even more financial trouble but he was real high, the ladies were very beautiful, and he felt like the women were celebrities after he found out the two of them were topless dancers.

Kool visited every day. He began exercising in the courtyard while I worked out. Josh, a pimp who also lived in the Motel, soon joined us. Josh shared a room with a beautiful young lady with a fantastic shape.

Every morning he would send her out to walk the streets. She returned at night with money, drugs, or both.

We began getting together as a group. Both men only smoked weed. All of the girls liked cocaine. We all enjoyed having philosophical conversations. Josh thought that I was a pimp because there were two women with me. I was never able to convince him that Mary was my legal wife and Mary Underwood was a long-time friend.

Kool soon ran out of dope and money. His stay at the motel had been nice, but it was time for him to make a move. In his mind, enough time had passed for Omar and Kojac to have forgotten the matter. He decided to go back to the Jungle to find out. In reality, two or three weeks had passed, but getting high interfered with Kool's ability to keep up with time. To him, months had gone by.

Kool went back into the Jungle, telling his customers that he had been out of town for a few months. It took all the nerve he had to go to Omar's apartment. However, he knew his life depended on him seeing Omar or Kojac before the hit men found him.

Kook took a deep breath and walked up the stairs to

Omar's door. He knocked lightly on the door. "It's open," Omar yelled from the inside. Kool hesitated. The door swung open, and Kool found himself facing a gun being held by Kojac.

"You got to be one of the world's biggest fools," Kojac said, as he placed the barrel on Kool's nose while he grabbed his shirt with the other hand and snatched him into the apartment. "You're supposed to be dead, you know. Now I know you're not stupid enough to come here unless you plan to pay me my money, including interest. Now pay up and die, fool."

The room was filled with nervous men looking at Kojac and Kool in amazement. "I got robbed," Kool said nervously. "Some gang from South Central, they beat me up and took my dope and my money. I been in the hospital for over three months. I can prove it. Come on, Kojac, please don't kill me."

"Go on and shoot him before he pisses on my floor," Omar said. "We got business to take care of."

"I don't want to be involved in no murder, Kojac," one of the men said. "All of us are ex-cons and you know we can't be nowhere near a gun. We came here to sell you guys some PCP, not to get involved in a fucking shooting. We can go while you handle your business. We can come back some other time."

"Hold off a minute, Kojac," Omar interrupted. "This fool may be of some use to us. What do you say we give him another chance? If he plays his cards right this time, he can pay us back and make some money for himself."

Kojac released Kool, took a deep breath to calm himself, then walked over to a man holding a briefcase in one hand, a gun in the other. "I'm sorry for the interruption. This is not the way we usually do business. Kool is one of our employees." He turned to Kool and motioned for him to take a seat. "We don't want to miss out on this opportunity. We've been looking for people who know how to make this PCP. The Lord works in mysterious ways, though. Me, Omar, Johnnie-Reb, none of us know a damned thing about angel dust so, we have no way of knowing if your product is the real thing. Maybe the Lord sent Kool to help us out."

Kojac turned to Kool. "These gentlemen deal in PCP; it's the stuff they use to make angel dust. We're new to the business, so we don't have a reliable way to test their product. I think you owe us one, Kool. Test the product for us, all is forgiven. If everything is OK, we can pay these good men and send them on their way."

"I've heard that PCP runs people crazy," Kool said nervously. "I don't want to mess around with that stuff."

"Would you rather be crazy or dead?" Kojac asked, without looking at Kool.

"All right, I'll do it."

Kojac nodded to one of the men. "Show us how the stuff works."

The man opened the briefcase and took out one of a few bottles of a clear liquid. The bottles were carefully wrapped. The man opened a bottle and inserted a dropper. He then unwrapped two small packets, one containing marijuana, the other spearmint leaves. He then filled the dropper with the liquid, placing a dropper full on the marijuana, another on the spearmint leaves. "It's called angel dust," the man said. "Some people get high with the liquid placed on the spearmint leaves, some like it on weed. They say the high is intensified when you put it on weed. Which one do you want to try?"

"Roll up a joint of each one," Kojac said. "Let him try them both."

Kool reluctantly took both joints. He lit one. The first

puff was enough to disrupt his thinking process. His actions indicated that he was completely stoned out of his mind. He sat staring at the ceiling, unable to speak or move. The men were laughing at his reactions.

Kool was unaware of anything else happening that night. Kojac had some of the men take him to his apartment where they threw him inside and he passed out on the floor. Once again, he had cheated the hit men. Omar paid the PCP dealers and made arrangements to do business with them in the future.

Angel dust sales went well in the Jungle. Kool got his job back, got himself out of debt and began to make money. He had also gained a fondness for angel dust. It was not long before he was smoking it with his female clients. Harriet loved it. Kool wanted to spend as much time with Harriet as he could. Harriet did not like Kool but she liked to get high and she could not afford it. She had three children and was on welfare.

Kool was busy telling everyone that Harriet was his girl. Harriet was just as busy telling everyone that she would never have sex with Kool, as he was telling people they were having sex all the time.

Harriet was a preacher's daughter. She had three children by Robert, who was now serving in the United States Army's Special Forces. She and her children's father planned to get married after he was discharged from the Army. His discharge had been delayed because of some trouble he had gotten into and he was now serving time in a military prison. He was soon to be released. Harriet kept an apartment for him.

Harriet and Robert had been together since high school. He was the captain of the football team. She was the head cheerleader. Robert was good-looking and well-built. Kool was not Harriet's type. Kool had a muscular build, but he wore thick eyeglasses and had crooked teeth. Had he not sold drugs, she would never associate with him. However, to keep the drugs coming, she had to make Kool believe she liked him, while she avoided having sex with him.

While they got high together quite often, she talked her way around Kool's sexual advances by teaching him about the Bible and telling him how her father raised her to be a good Christian. "I already have three children, so you can see I can't afford to make any mistakes," she would say. "Besides, I'm lucky enough to be engaged to their father, I'm not going to do anything to jeopardize that." Kool felt like as long as she liked to get high, there was always a chance. Besides, he loved to talk. He often told people, "I was blessed with the gift of gab. I can talk anyone into anything and talk my way out of anything."

Nitro worked at the Page Four Lounge. He was a well-known bouncer. He told everyone that he was an ex-prizefighter and that was exactly what he looked like. He was big, musclebound, had facial scars and a front tooth missing. He always wore a suit and tie. He regularly dated girls who came into the bar and regularly bought marijuana and cocaine from Kool.

Nitro considered Kool a weak man and began taking advantage. He began getting drugs on credit. After credit was established, he began to pay late, or not at all. Kool mistakenly told Nitro that he was short on money and could not afford to get in trouble with Kojac again. Nitro offered to help him out by sharing his apartment and splitting the rent. Instead of getting paid for his drugs, Kool ended up accepting Nitro's money as rent with a promise that the drugs would be paid for later. Nitro then had the key to Kool's apartment. He never paid for the drugs and never paid rent again.

Nitro did not show up at the apartment often. He claimed he owned a big house in the valley and only spent the night at Kool's apartment when he did not feel like driving home or when he had met some lady at the bar and needed the place for a quickie.

Kool had managed to pay for his drugs for months. Keeping Harriet high and being unable to collect from Nitro, things were beginning to take a turn for the worse. Just like before, it was time to pay and he was short. He told Harriet that he would get into trouble if he did not come up with the money. Harriet promised she would help him pay. The money never materialized.

To make matters worse, Nitro showed up at the apartment with two women who wanted to get high. Kool was not home. Nitro tore the place apart, found Kool's drugs, and helped himself. Nitro had never used angel dust before. The first taste sent him straight into another world. He could not speak or understand anything or anyone. He went in to a zombie-like state and the girls could not bring him around. They eventually called 911. Nitro was rushed off to the hospital. He was later placed in a mental facility, where he remained in the zombie-like state for over a month.

Kool was pleased that he once again had his apartment to himself. The problem was there was no way to talk Kojac out of killing him this time. Kool hid out in his apartment. He did not answer the door or phone. He felt like his luck had finally run out. He constantly peeked out of his window to see if the enforcers were coming. He saw me passing his apartment one day, and began to notice that I passed his place early each morning and returned late in the day.

Kool decided to disguise himself and follow me to my apartment one evening when I returned from my daily walk. I was limping badly as I walked up the stairs to my door. I had noticed someone following me. Thinking it was a robbery attempt, I got ready to defend myself.

"Twenty-five," he called from the bottom of the stairs, trying to conceal himself.

"Who is it?" I answered.

"Kool. It's Kool, man. Remember me, we met at the Adams Motel, you're the karate man, you do that tae kwon do stuff."

"I remember, you're the dope man. Why are you disguising yourself.?"

"People are after me. Open the door and let's get inside."

Kool followed me inside. It was just about to get dark. There was no electricity in my apartment. I lit a candle as he looked around in the dark for a seat.

"How long have you been here?" he asked.

"About three or four months."

"Where are those two beautiful women who were with you? Those two go-go dancers, Mary and Mary?"

"Gone, both gone. Mary Underwood went back to Detroit shortly after you and I met at the motel. My wife and I moved into this apartment together, but she left."

"I live right up the street. I've been living here for years. I have the best view in the Jungle. From my apartment, I can see everything that comes in or out. I've been seeing you take long walks, leaving early in the morning, coming home near dark."

"I'm trying to walk off depression and I am training myself to walk again."

"What happened? The last time I saw you, you were doing the tae kwon do thing."

"I was recovering from foot surgery when we moved here. I must have done some damage by working out too soon. My foot began to hurt at the motel. The pain eventually got so bad I could not walk at all. This was shortly after you left the motel."

"Sounds like your luck is about as bad as mine. Things were going good for me for a while. I met this fine bitch named Harriet . . . She's light-skinned like your wife . . . We had it going on until I got into money trouble with the gang."

"Fine women come in all colors. Light-skinned seems to mean a lot to you."

"Color means everything in this country. I love high-yellow bitches, but high-yellow or not, all women are bitches. That's just the way it is."

"That is why you never married. If you don't respect women, they won't respect you."

"You don't know bitches like I do. They are all yours, as long as you are the man with the money. When the money's gone, the bitches are gone."

Kool's words awakened memories of my life in Detroit. I had worked in the automobile factory for the Chrysler corporation. The guys on the job would tease me about my engagement to Mary. "You know that woman is too fine for your ugly ass," my friends would say. "She won't be with you for long."

My problem was that I was afraid they were right. I was a poor country boy from Alabama. My wife-to-be was well-known as one of the finest dancers in Detroit. I had always felt that Mary was way too classy for me. I had been taught to respect my elders, though, and I always listened to the older, wiser men. Old man Reed was the wise man on the job; his advice calmed my fears. He would come to my rescue by saying, "You may not keep her long, but at least you can say you had her."

My life in Detroit had been magical. In the eight

years I lived there, I had been transformed from a dumb country bumpkin into a well-known martial arts instructor and ladies' man. I had dated what seemed like hundreds of dancers before I asked Mary to marry me.

"Believe me," I said to Kool, "If it's one thing I know, it's women. Mary and I had the perfect marriage. Then, my first wife Minnie managed to get me tied up in the court system with a child-support case. I ended up in jail, wondering how in the hell I got there. Everything went downhill after that. That's how we ended up out here."

"You running from the cops in Detroit?"

"Yeah," I answered. In the environment I had encountered since my arrival in Los Angeles, I did not feel it wise to say I actually came to join the Los Angeles Police Department. I had applied for the position of police officer in Detroit and Los Angeles. I had passed the written and physical test in Detroit before being told I had a child-support problem that needed to be straightened out. Finding it impossible to satisfy the Court, I decided to test in Los Angeles.

"I'm a hustler," Kool said. "I been hustling all my life. I'm always on the run. If the cops are not after me, the gangsters are. I'm going to get out of this life one day, though. I go to school on the GI bill. I plan to get my degree and one of them high-paying jobs. I wish I could pimp though. I know a pimp named Blue, he has this blue pimped-out Cadillac. Almost everything in his apartment is blue and I just can't describe the bitches, talk about fine."

"I could never be a pimp. I love fine women, but I'm too jealous to share them with other men. I don't care how many women I have, I don't want them with anyone but me."

"Well, it ain't good to be up in here without lights,

gas, and furniture. I can turn you on to Omar and Kojac if you want me to. They are the gang bosses in the Jungle. I can't introduce you personally right now, but I can tell you how to get in touch. You let them know you're on the run from the cops, they'll put you to work. You could sling some dope until you get on your feet."

"I don't want to sell no dope. It's bad karma; besides, I was doing OK working. I made a good living teaching martial arts and working for Chrysler. I lived just as good as the pimps and drug dealers. I never had to do anything that would get me put into prison, and I'm too old to start now. When I get well, I'll get another job. I ain't no criminal."

"Shit, nigger, you can't survive here unless you are with some gang. We are all gang members; we don't have a choice. They already took you off the job and put you in jail. If working was the way out, there wouldn't be so many Black men in prison. The system is set up that way. For Blacks and Mexicans it's hustle or die."

"Not me, I worked for Chrysler for seven years. Before that, I worked for the federal government. Besides that, I'm a Vietnam veteran. I believe my situation will be straightened out soon."

"How long before they evict you?"

"I don't know."

"The last time we met you didn't get high. Do you now?"

"No."

"You will before this is over," Kool said as he got up to leave. He took out a bag of weed and two joints of angel dust. He threw them to me. "You might need these. I'll see you later. You already live like an animal, no lights or gas, soon they'll put you out and you won't have a roof over your head. It may take that for you to see how the system really works. Here's something for you to think about while you're doing your daily meditation. Pimp or die, nigger."

Dying was exactly what I was prepared to do, I thought as Kool left.

The events leading up to my being there were too weird to explain. The only thing that I was certain about was things were totally out of my control. I could not get rid of the fear that I had come to Los Angeles to die. I felt that my karma had forced me there, and there was no way to avoid my death.

After the pain in my foot got so bad that I could no longer work at the motel, we moved into the apartment and I applied for unemployment compensation. The State of California ruled that I should be penalized thirteen weeks of my benefits because I voluntarily quit my job with Chrysler. I was ordered to come back in thirteen weeks. At the end of the thirteen weeks, our lights and gas had been turned off. I went back to the unemployment office to be told, "We meant for you to report to the office each week during the thirteen-week penalty period." Because I had not reported back each week, my benefits were denied and all I could do was request a hearing.

I could not reapply for unemployment or apply for work because the pain in my foot had made it impossible for me to walk. I was sent to a doctor to be examined for state disability. The doctor looked at my physical build, and became offended. "What's the reason you're disabled?" he asked.

"It's my foot," I answered. "I recently had surgery and the foot never healed. Standing is very painful right now."

"If you can't stand and work, you can sit and work.

You are in too good a shape to be on disability. That'll be all."

Mary and I were completely out of money by that time. Mary wanted to get a job at the Page-Four Lounge to keep us from starving to death. I did not agree. I did not want her back in the bars. We had agreed that she would stop when we were married.

Since my disability was due to a foot injury I received while serving in the United States Marine Corps, I wrote to President Carter about our situation. The Veterans Administration and the American Legion were contacted. The American Legion brought us some food and paid two weeks' rent. The Legion was sure I would be receiving compensation from the Veterans Administration during the two-week period. They were wrong. After the two weeks were over and the Veterans Administration had not responded, the landlord was upset, because, according to him, the American Legion would have paid a month or more if I had been a white veteran.

Mary took the job at the Page Four Lounge, but my inability to walk and her getting high and partying with her fellow employees soon got us into arguments. We thought things were changing for the better with the assistance from the American Legion. However, instead of a veteran, the Veterans Administration treated me like an enemy of the state. Finding ourselves without any means of support, Mary became paranoid. Soon, she spent of her time getting high with her friends from the Page Four Lounge. Eventually she moved in with a girlfriend.

Finding myself unable to walk and being alone in a dark cold apartment made me realize that, if I did not help myself, I would die. I had reached the point where I wanted to die. I did not want to go to hell. Life here on earth had been too hard. There was no way I would risk going to a worse place. The thought prevented me from committing suicide. I had been taught that suicide was one sure way of going to hell.

I realized that, no matter how painful, I had to make myself walk again. I began to leave early each morning and walk as far as I could. I began reliving a time when I had been ordered to walk on an injured foot while in the Marine Corps. I went to the doctor after injuring my ankle. The doctor placed me on light duty. My commanding officer refused to honor the doctor's orders for me. In addition he said that he was determined to teach me to function while in pain. While my foot was injured, I was ordered to carry an M-60 machine gun everywhere I went while I was on the base. This included ten-mile marches to the range. While the other Marines relieved each other every three miles, I was made to carry the gun alone the entire ten miles, both ways.

The words of my Commanding Officer turned out to be true. "Marines have to learn to ignore pain," He would say. "I want you to carry that weapon everywhere you go. When you march to the range, your Fire Team is not to relieve each other, you carry the weapon the whole ten miles. Soon you'll learn to function without thinking about your feet hurting. One day your life may depend on it." After training, I was ordered to stand at attention for hours at a time.

I had carried around a lot of hate for my commanding officer. Now, I could not help but appreciate how I had been trained. Otherwise I may have died alone in that empty apartment trapped by the pain in my foot. I thought about my Marine Corps training each day. I walked, in pain for miles and miles each day. I came back and practiced martial arts at night until I passed out. I was on one of those walks when Kool saw me.

I had heard about angel dust. I had been afraid to try it. After Kool left the joints I began to wonder if I would lose my mind or even die if I smoked one of the joints. Either way, it would mean an escape from the extreme depression and pain I was in. I lit the angel dust, I did not lose my thought process, but I found myself pain-free for the first time in years.

Kool began to drop by often. He would bring fresh stolen bread and for a while that was all I had to eat. He would also supply drugs, and we sat there in the dark, got high, and talked about the Bible, philosophy, and martial arts.

One day Kool came by excited about what he thought was the answer to his financial problems. He held a stack of government checks he had stolen from the mailman. "Look at this shit!" he said, unable to control his excitement. "I'm rich."

"Where did you get them?" I asked.

"The mailman was putting mail in one of the apartments on Coliseum. I passed that little mail cart and saw this big stack of welfare checks, I just looked around to see if anyone was looking. Then, swoop, I took the whole stack. You want some?"

"No thanks. I would have no way to cash them, and getting caught with one would be a federal offense. I told you, I'm not a criminal. How you going to cash them?"

"I don't know, I'm going to give Omar and Kojac a stack to clear up my debt. Then, I'll give the rest to this pimp, he'll let his bitches cash them."

Kool took the checks to Omar and Kojac. They did not accept the checks for payment, but his attempt to pay saved his life once again. They gave him a week to cash the checks and bring them the money.

Kool went to Blue for help. Blue refused the stolen

checks. Another pimp agreed to take the checks for sixty percent of the value. Unable to get other offers, Kool had to accept. He gave the pimp the checks. He was told to come back in a couple of days for the money. Each day for a week, the pimp told Kool to return the next day. Kool ended up getting less than five hundred dollars for the entire stack of checks. In addition, the week had passed and the contract on his life was on again. Omar had everyone in the Jungle looking for Kool. It became too dangerous for him to visit me.

I had not eaten in a few days when I began to write President Carter again. The President had the Veterans Administration arrange a physical examination for me. I remember the expression of the hospital worker when he asked me to undress for a physical. I heard the man's comment to the doctor before he came into the room. "This guy should be ashamed to talk about pain. You should see the stomach muscles on him. This guy is as hard as a rock." Again, a doctor was so impressed with my physique that there was no way he was helping me get disability. Once again, without any examination, the doctor said that I was OK. My disability claim was again denied.

The State of California sent information about a medical card I could get from the County Welfare Office. With the card I got a chance to see a podiatrist. The doctor examined the foot and took x-rays. He informed me that the pain was due to some type of metal wire the doctor had placed in my toe during the surgery. He felt that it was some type of clamp that had been used when too much bone had been removed from my foot.

The doctor also wrote a letter, addressed "To whom it may concern," bluntly stating that I was getting the runaround from the Veterans Administration about my disability. The letter was like a gift from God to me. I sent a copy to President Carter.

In order to eat, I began pushing a shopping cart and picking up cans to sell. The first time, I spent five hours picking up cans and two hours pushing the basket to the aluminum dealer to find that most of the cans I had were not aluminum. I collected less than two dollars for my work, but I got back to the apartment with a loaf of bread and a can of beans. I began picking up the cans every day. After the letter from the podiatrist reached President Carter's office, the President arranged for another medical examination.

I was apprehensive about my next visit to the Veterans Administration Hospital. This time however, an angel came to the rescue. This beautiful Indian lady came into the room with a long thick braid that fell to her knees. Three male doctors followed her. The lady began to examine my feet; she looked around at the men in amazement. "He has the problems he described," she said.

The men looked at each other as if they were embarrassed, then they looked at my feet. They hesitated for a moment then. All of them began to make examinations. There was an agreement that I was disabled. The case would now be sent to a rating board to determine the compensation amount.

The employees of the Veterans Administration seemed to have been angered by my writing to President Carter and by the doctor's letter about them giving me "the runaround." I expected the least amount of compensation the government could pay, if any. This would be their way of getting even. The Iran hostage crisis happened. President Carter had to turn his attention to much more important things.

Two
The Coldest Days

I found myself afraid to open my eyes when I woke up in the mornings. I was still hoping everything was a bad dream, and wishing I could wake up and find everything back to normal. My fear that I had come to Los Angeles to die had become more intense.

Without lights, a radio, or television, all I could do was think. My life kept flashing before me. Nothing I had done in my life should have led me to where I was. In the world that was normal for me, Mary would be in another room talking on the phone. On Wednesdays I'd teach my martial arts class. Every other day, except for Sunday, I was in the school training under other instructors. Grand master Shim taught on Sundays. His classes were always filled. I never missed a class.

I had worked seven years with the Chrysler Corp., beginning in 1980. Most of that time we were on a six- or seven-day schedule. Everyone knew that I was a martial arts fanatic. I was teased a lot about the number of years I had trained. "I know you have been training for over seven years," some would say. "If you haven't learned it all by now, you can forget it."

If I missed a day's work, I would return to face the guys joking about me trying to use martial arts in some bar fight and losing. I worked for Chrysler for seven years before leaving for Los Angeles. I had trained with grand master Shim for the same number of years. Before that, I worked for the Veterans Administration in Detroit, transferring there from the Veterans Administration regional office in Montgomery, Alabama.

The transfer was due to a failed marriage. Minnie and I were nineteen years old when we got married; my son Percy was born about nine months after the marriage. In less than a year we were separated. Minnie took our son Percy to Detroit. I moved to Detroit to take part in my son's upbringing. Minnie got married again to a guy named Rudy.

In Detroit, my girlfriend Liz moved in with me. We never got married but lived as husband and wife. My daughter Carla was born. I worked as a file clerk with Detroit's Veterans Administration Office. I looked like a government worker. I kept the Marine Corps haircut. My dress was always a white shirt and tie. Liz would never allow me to dress any other way. All of my spare time was spent practicing martial arts.

The Chrysler corporation paid more money than the government. When the job at Chrysler became available, I worked both jobs as long as I could. Liz began to complain about my never being at home. Liz and I had met and began an affair when we both worked for the Veterans Administration in Alabama. We kept in touch when I moved to Detroit, and eventually she moved to Detroit. She had family there. When we met, Liz was already engaged to James Harris, a career marine. Our affair started while he was overseas. We fell in love. Liz never meant to end her relationship with James or to get pregnant.

When the complaints began about me working too much, I would explain that I was planning for my children's futures. I would offer to send her on a trip to Alabama. I felt like being around her family for a while would cheer her up. Eventually I began to see that the complaints would always occur whenever James Harris was on leave in Alabama. Liz knew how to trick me into sending her on trips to see James.

It was while she was on one of those trips, I was introduced to a stripper named Apache by my brother Ace. Ace was dating Mae. Mae was a friend of Apache. Apache was looking for someone to date. She had been having an affair with a wealthy married man. The affair had gone on for years and she was not willing to end it. The man supported her child and paid her bills. Apache was the first dancer I dated. She explained to me that she was only interested in a sex partner. It was hard to believe that I could be that lucky.

Apache loved sex more than anyone I ever heard about or read about. Her performances would sometimes get her arrested. Because she made a lot of money for the clubs, the owners would immediately bail her out to get her back to work. On some occasions she went to jail twice on the same night.

She changed my whole world. She was far more beautiful than any woman I ever dreamed I could be with. She was fifteen years older than me and pleased with my inexperience. She began to spend a lot of time educating me about sex.

After our affair began, I began trying to get Liz to go on trips more frequently and to stay longer. The two women I loved both had other lovers, yet I was very happy. Apache would constantly ask for money but I never gave up more than I could afford. A lot of the guys who worked at Chrysler had been to see her shows and I became popular when everyone found out I was dating her.

Everything went well until I came home one night to find Liz had moved out and taken all of the furniture out of the apartment. James Harris had retired from the Marines. Liz had found an apartment for them to live together. I was angry at first, but I had been working and saving for a long time. It was easy to replace the furniture. I did locate her to make sure our daughter Carla was OK. It was after she had moved in with James that Liz found out she was pregnant with our daughter Raquel.

James did not adjust to life outside of the Marine Corps. He turned out to be an alcoholic. There was never a time when he was not drunk. Liz ended the relationship and went on welfare. She informed me that the county would not accept applications for welfare unless the mother had opened a child-support case against he father. She felt that it would be unfair to open a child-support case since I had always supported the children. I told her that I did not mind paying and I went to the court to voluntarily have payments taken from my paychecks.

It was just me and Apache then, except for the fact that, every once in a while, she felt obligated to spend time with her wealthy married man. Things began to change with Apache when Ernestine began working at the club. Ernestine was fifteen years younger than Apache. She was lovelier than any of the other girls. She had huge breasts and, for some reason, she liked me.

When Apache saw Ernestine and I getting close, our relationship changed. Suddenly, she no longer asked me for money. Now she began spending money on me. Apache and Ernestine got into a competition buying me clothes and jewelry. My white-shirt-and-tie look began to fade.

The strippers changed me. Where I would have been

afraid to try to talk to them before, I found myself dating them, a lot of them. I picked up the name Twenty-five from the girls. They began instructing me on how to wear my hair. Soon my hair fell below my shoulders. The ladies picked all of my clothes. As time passed, I began to look like a pimp. Adding to my image was the fact that there were always new dancers. Each time I thought I had seen the most beautiful one, someone more beautiful would appear.

I wore stylish suits, coats, shoes, and hats. I hated loud colors, though. I only wore black, brown, dark blue, and gray. Beginning with Apache as a sex instructor, I was transformed from a country bumpkin into a player. My obsessive practice of martial arts kept the women interested. Bruce Lee was becoming popular. Girls were interested in marital arts and martial artists. I could not have been happier. I had good friends at grand master Shim's martial arts school and good friends at Chrysler.

Guys liked to hang around me because wherever I was there were always beautiful girls. "I don't understand it," my friend Rob would say, shaking his head. "You ain't by no means no good-looking nigger. I just can't see why those women are so crazy about you."

"Some of us have what women like, some don't. I'm just blessed to be one of those they like. Besides, they know I love them," I would say. "I'm just like the good Shepherd. If one of my ladies wanders off, I leave all the others until I get her back."

"Twenty-five, you're a fool," the guys would say. "One of these days, you'll run into the wrong woman. Then you'll be sorry." We were always laughing and joking on the job. I worked the evening shift. I was in martial arts class every morning. I was in the bars every night. I was always bragging to the guys at work about my adventures.

Things went on like that for years. Then, it was like I had sold my soul for seven years of pleasure and, the seven years were up. Everything began to change. The girls I had been dating long-term with no strings attached, began to talk about getting married. Even Apache began questioning me about marriage. I was having the time of my life meeting, dating, and sleeping with some of God's most beautiful creations. Then, as was bound to happen, I began to run into the wrong women.

I met Angel one night when I visited a bar called the Kaweka Lounge. I was dressed in black. A dancer/waitress approached me as I took a seat at the bar. "Mister," she said, "you look like a gangster."

"Just goes to show you, looks can be deceiving. I'm not a gangster. In fact, I'm a preacher."

She laughed. "If you're a preacher, what are you doing in a place like, this?"

"Spreading the word baby, spreading the word." Someone called for a drink, and she had to leave. I turned to the stage, which was behind the bar. I looked into the eyes of Angel for the first time. Angel was her name and she looked like an Angel. Our eyes met and we stared at each other while she danced. She then made this fantastic leap from the stage to the bar. She landed right in front of me. I was trying hard to maintain my cool image, but it was hard to hide my excitement. Angel danced the entire record right in front of me. The men were yelling in the background while I sat there looking up between her legs. I bought her a drink after her dance. We began to date.

Other dancers began telling me to be careful with Angel. She was into things most of them did not do. I still had some of my Alabama dumbness, so I was not aware of certain things about Angel. One thing was, there was usually an older guy at the bar on the nights she danced. She told me it was her father and I never thought twice about it. I later found out that the man was her pimp.

Angel and I got real close before I found out that she was a heroin addict. I explained to her that I had no education about hard drugs. I only knew they were bad news. I informed her that I did not want to date anyone on heroin. I did not end the relationship in time, though.

Angel's pimp had become angered by our relationship. She had been sneaking out to see me against his wishes. I came home from work one night to find Angie lying in front of my apartment door. She was beaten so badly she was unrecognizable. I got her treated at the emergency room and took her to my apartment to recuperate. I was more afraid than I had ever been. If I did not do something, the pimp would have the impression that he punked me out. For the first time since I began taking martial arts, I went to use it. I told my friend Robert Humphrey what I was about to do. We had trained together for several years. He promised to watch my back.

The pimp frequented a bar on Grand River Ave. Humphrey was already inside when I arrived. There was one man seated at a table alone behind the pimp. That guy was watching his back. A big guy who looked like a fighter sat at the table with him; he was a bodyguard.

I walked in and headed straight for the table. The big guy got up as I approached. He held out his hands to warn me to stay away. He was about to speak when I grabbed his arm and executed two roundhouse kicks to his ribs, then one to his head. He fell to the floor unconscious.

The man at the back table got up, reaching inside his coat for his gun. Humphrey tapped him on the shoulder and I knocked him out with a spinning heel kick when he turned around. The pimp got up, reaching inside his coat. I kicked the table over on him. He fell, dropping the weapon. I helped him up and knocked him down again. He leaped to his feet and grabbed a chair. I kicked the chair into him knocking him down. I kept picking him up and knocking him down until he stayed down crying and begging. I walked out.

My next unpleasant experience was with Pat. Pat had the most beautiful legs I had ever seen. We dated for a while and got along well. She and her five-year-old son moved in with me. Pat was obsessed with pimps. She was delighted that I had the appearance of a pimp and some thought that I was a pimp. The thing that was upsetting to me was she wanted her son to grow up to be a pimp. She dressed the five-year-old in pimp-like suits, had his ear pierced, got him a perm, and put gold watches and rings on the child. The child was very disobedient. On one occasion I yelled at the child because he would not stop kicking me. Pat told me that he was not my child and I had no right to discipline him. I asked her to move.

After a bad experience with a set of identical twins, I swore that my life as a player was over.

When I met Brenda, I was amazed at how a woman her size could have such huge breasts, then I turned to see an exact duplicate of her, her sister Linda. Brenda and I began to date; Linda was married. I was trying to get them both in bed together. I sincerely wanted to be able to brag about sleeping with identical twins. Linda wanted to; Brenda did not. She was ready to get married and settle down, she wanted to keep her self-respect.

I wandered into the bar one night when Brenda was off. Linda told me she about to get off and wanted to go bar-hopping with me. We ended up in my apartment. I was afraid to bring up sex because I felt like she would tell her sister. We ended up sleeping together. I could now brag that I had slept with identical twins, but things did not end there.

Sex with Linda turned out to be much more exciting than with her twin. We began to see each other behind Brenda's back, and behind Linda's husband's back. Linda's husband caught us kissing once in her dressing room. I began to drop Brenda off at home after our dates, and sneak over to pick up Linda, who was sneaking out on her husband. I did not like the sneaking; it was hard to brag about my accomplishment.

Peaches was the barmaid. She informed Brenda that her twin sister was cheating on her husband with Brenda's boyfriend. Brenda went to confront her sister who was at the time at my apartment. My heart sank when I answered the door to find Brenda. I found myself feeling lower than I had ever felt, telling Brenda I could not let her in because I had company. I can never forget the sad look on her face, knowing her twin sister was there.

After that incident, guilt kept me from dating anyone for a while. Before, everything had been fun; now, I had to seriously think about what I was doing. Aside from having something to brag about with the guys, dating a lot of women was only causing problems and wasting time. My plans were to devote all of my spare time to marital arts, date only one woman, go to school, and try to make something of myself. I began spending more time with my children.

I always picked my son Percy up from his grandmother's house. Minnie and I had not seen each other or made contact in over five years. The children bragging about my penthouse apartment made Minnie want to see where I lived. She was impressed enough to think that I had become wealthy. Percy had been born in Alabama, and, at the age of five, the court refused Minnie's attempts to get increased support payments. I had not met her husband and I was unaware that that the two of them had a child together (named Antoine). I also did not know that her husband's child had been given my last name.

It was shortly after Minnie's visit to my apartment that I received an order to come to court. The judge asked why I had not been supporting Antoine, along with the rest of my children. My answer was, "I never heard of Antoine." This made the judge think I was attempting to be disrespectful. I stood there in shock, both about the child and that the judge thought Minnie and I were still married. I looked real stupid. Minnie was praying that I could not explain the situation to the judge, and I could not.

The judge gave an order for me to pay support for Antoine. I did my best to explain that I did not know Antoine, I had not seen Minnie in over five years, so I could not be the father, and money was being deducted from my paychecks for my own children. I told the judge that there was no way I could pay what he asked.

The Friend of the Court represented Minnie. The representative actually lied about my salary. The report given to the judge was based on the overtime I had worked. The judge said he did not believe me. I also made a request for a blood test. The judge became angry and said, "If you don't agree to pay this money, you're going to jail." I told him I had no way of paying the money. I was immediately sent to jail.

I knew that my incarceration was not legal. I mistakenly thought that it was an attempt by the judge to scare me. I expected to be released after a few hours. I was due at work. After I had spent the night, I realized I was in trouble. I did not know why I had been locked up or how long I was to be locked up. After the first night, I was sent to maximum security, because the other cells were full. I spent a few days there getting to know killers and rapists. I was later sent to the Detroit House of Corrections. During the time I stayed there, all I could think about was killing the judge. Minnie had lied, however. Nothing she said was checked out, and no one listened to me.

There was trouble at the house of corrections on the first day. We were given a lecture on returning the sheet, towels, and pillowcases assigned to us. Everything had to be returned before we got out, we were told. I arrived at my bed to find everything gone. I was looking around for the thing I was supposed to have, when two men approached me about buying some sheets. They informed me again that I needed those things before I got out. If I did not purchase the bedding from them, my release would be delayed.

My anger had grown every day I had been incarcerated. "I was just told that I would find sheets, pillowcases and towels on my bed, they are not here, and you guys somehow have the stuff to sell? I think the stuff is mine, and I want it back on my bed right away."

"We got us a tough guy," one of them said, just before I kicked him in the mouth. The other man attacked me, and I began going from one to the other, punching and kicking. I was about to inflict serious injuries when some of the other guys pulled me away, warning me that I was going to kill them.

I recovered my sheet and towels and, from then on, no one bothered me. Guys would ask me questions about my martial arts. I tried to keep my sanity by working out. I could not bring myself to relax. I had grown up determined to stay away from crime, to avoid going to jail. I could not accept being incarcerated for nothing. I found it embarrassing to say I was incarcerated because of child support. I convinced myself that I would rather be in prison for killing the judge.

I could hear a train go by every day. I made up my mind to escape. It was raining really hard on the day I decided to go over the fence. About an hour before I was set to go, my name was called over the speaker. I was thinking someone had told the guards about my escape plan.

I got to the office to find out someone was there to bail me out. I was so happy I could not stop the tears. Luckily, it was raining too hard for anyone to notice that I was crying. Some of the guys were able to see who was picking me up. It was Pat. She was driving her Cadillac. She was wearing a white jumpsuit with splits in the side. She was a beautiful woman, but now, she looked like an angel. "Pimp on!" the men were saying. Everyone was running to the gate to see Pat. The guards and the inmates were going crazy. Some of them began to walk up to me in a hypnotic state and offer me cigarettes.

Pat said that she found out I was locked up, and she got the money to get me out. She wanted to get together later to talk about our failed relationship. I never had any problems with Pat. I did explain that it was too hard to deal with a five-year-old child that she wanted to turn into a pimp. We made a date to meet at a club called Johnnie's Dream Bar in downtown Detroit. I thought that I had covered all of the bars in Detroit, but I had never been to that one. Pat and I were having a drink when Mary walked in.

At first glance, I fell in love with Mary. I could not get my mind off her the entire night. All I could think about was getting back to that bar alone so that I could talk to her. I came back a few nights later. I was surprised when Mary approached me at the pinball machine. "You broke my record," she said.

"Pardon me?" I replied. "I'm a pinball freak," she said. "I have the highest score on each of these machines. You broke my record and now I have to challenge you to a game." We became friends over the pinball machines. Later we began to date.

With Mary, life was like a never-ending party. The guys at work would go crazy when Mary and some of the other dancers would bring me to work and pick me up. I talked her into joining grand master Shim's classes. We trained in the mornings, worked in the evenings, and partied at night. Our weekends were spent with children. Mary loved children—my children, Percy, Carla, and Raquel, and Mary's nieces and nephew, Juanita, Teresa and Nate. Before long, we had made wedding plans.

Our wedding plans had been made when, on payday, my supervisor at Chrysler informed me that the court had taken my entire paycheck. I did not know what was happening but I was confident that I would be paid the next week. Each week the supervisor would tell me that the court had taken my check. It never stopped. It was hard to explain working all those hours and not bring home a check. My thoughts were, they know I have to have some means to survive, eventually they have to let me have some of my salary. They never stopped taking all of my check.

I went to the court to explain my situation. The court informed me that there was nothing I could do. The judge's ruling was final. Our friends began recommending lawyers. None of them would take the case. Mary and I covered the phone book without success. We did not realize at the time that lawyers avoided child-support cases. There was no way I could have the case examined to show that mistakes had been made. I became very depressed.

Mary had her problems too. She had not told me that Pat had been making threatening calls. She had been telling Mary that we were still going together and that we were together when she thought I was at work. Not receiving a paycheck made the stories believable.

An old man who owned a liquor store on Woodard Avenue had offered me a chance to earn five thousand fighting in his after-hours joint. I had turned him down before but I desperately needed money at that time. I accepted the fight and won the money. The money carried me for a while, but I was still working every day with no income.

On one occasion, Pat called me and said she needed money desperately. She had paid to get me out of jail, and I owed her. I told her that I had not been getting paid and my savings were just about gone. However, I had a few dollars left from the five thousand,. I could let her have a few dollars if she was in trouble. I was to meet her at the bar where she danced.

When I got to the bar where she worked, two bug guys were waiting for me in the parking lot. Pat had paid them to beat me up. I needed the fight to work off the anger. I knocked both the men out, then went inside to find Pat. She had left town. Before she left, she had called Mary and told her that she and I were about to have a rendezvous. She informed Mary that I would be taking money out of my account and bringing it to her. Mary was aware that I had taken money from my account. I was angry, but I could not help but admire the scheme.

Shortly after that incident, I went into the hospital for foot surgery. During the time I was recuperating, the children visited every day. I smiled thinking about Mary yelling at the children, "Stop jumping on the bed, you are going to hurt his foot." The children were hurting my foot. However; they were having so much fun, I was not complaining.

These were memories of the last weekend I spent with my children. I was just getting back on my feet when we got a visit from a detective with the Detroit Police. The visit was about a five-year-old application I had filed with the Detroit Police. The detective said that black men who filed applications during the same period were denied positions because of their race. The federal government had ordered the Department to look up some of these men and ask if they were still interested in becoming policemen. I told him that I was.

I passed all of the tests and got through the oral interview before being told by a captain that I had to straighten things out with the Friend of the Court. I went to the court to find out what I could do to get things straightened out. I was told that, "When a Judge makes a ruling, it can't be changed." I explained that my whole paycheck was being taken, and the case was preventing me from getting a position with the Police Department. If I could have blood test, I could prove that I was not the father of the child named in the case. No one would believe that I had been denied a blood test. No one would believe the court had made any errors in the case.

When I got the notice to test for the Los Angeles Police, I had no choice but to try. It had become impossible for me to earn a living in Detroit. I went to see grand master Shim before I left. I had trained with him for over seven years. I felt bad about having to leave. "Life can make many unexpected turns," grand master Shim said. "No matter what happens, you work out two hours every morning and two hours every night. If you do that, you'll never be a loser."

I could not leave without visiting some of the clubs I had frequented to say my goodbyes to the girls. I had made my last stop at a bar on Woodward Avenue. I was saying good-bye to Princess, a long time friend when a fight broke out over a game of pool. A man was knocked over my table. Princess and I got up quickly, trying to avoid the drinks that were spilled. The owner pulled his shotgun and pointed it at two big guys who were beating up on one little guy. The men told the owner to put the gun away, they were leaving.

They came over to my table, as Princess and I were helping the little guy to his feet. "We'll be waiting for you outside man," one of the men said.

"He's kind of small," I said. "Why don't you just leave him alone?"

"This ain't your business, man," one of the men replied. "If I were you, I'd keep talking to this beautiful lady. That way, you won't get fucked up along with this punk."

"I'll walk you to your car, man," I said to the little man, ignoring the two big guys.

"Oh, we got us one of them bad muther-fuckers," one of the men replied.

"Wait!" the other man said. "I know him, that's Twenty-five, the karate man. He's the one who fucked up that pimp, Cadillac Herb."

"We're out of here," his partner replied. "We'll get you later, Rudy."

After the two men left, the little man thanked me for my help. He asked if he could buy me a drink. I was about to leave, I told him.

"I know you," the man said. "You're Percy's father."

"How do you know my son?" I asked.

"I've seen you before when you came to pick up Percy from his Grandmother's. You've seen me there with Minnie's brother Frank, you just don't remember."

"Well, good luck, man, you take care of yourself," I turned to Princess.

"Wait!" the man said. "My name is Rudy. You're not supposed to know this, but I have to tell you because you helped me out. Minnie and I are married. We were married nearly six years ago. I know how she got you messed up with the court."

I thanked Rudy for the information, but it meant nothing to me. I was finished trying to deal with the courts in Detroit. I would try to find a lawyer in Los Angeles who would handle my wrongful incarceration case.

In Los Angeles, I passed the written test for police officer. I was told I failed the oral interview by one point. At first I was told my status as a service-connected Disabled Veteran allowed me the points I needed to pass the interview. I was sent to get proof that I was a Disabled Veteran. When I returned with the proof, I was told the points were not allowed until the test was passed.

Mary and I began working at the motel until I began having problems from my foot surgery. From there, we had moved to the Jungle. We did not know it was called the Jungle, we were just looking for a Black neighborhood. The apartments there were pretty nice. I had resigned myself to the reality that I had come there to die. I knew I had not lived a good life, I was in a hurry to get it over with. I prayed that Mary would get out of there in one piece.

In the apartment, I became aware of how poor people get hooked on drugs. When Kool had provided me the drug, I knew how it felt to be both mentally relaxed and pain-free. Drugs could actually take your mind away from all your problems for a while the only thing was, when the high left, the problems returned. I realized the trip away from my problems was temporary. However, as is the case with an addict, the need to get away from reality was more important than anything else.

Without drugs, I could not get rid of the pounding headaches, uncontrollable anxiety, the mad rush of my life flashing before me, or the stabbing pain in my foot.

I followed grand master Shim's advice. I worked out morning and night. I tried to tire myself out enough to sleep. Each day it took more and more exercise. I kept trying harder because I dreaded being awake.

The pounding in my head must have been my blood pressure gone way up. I was lying there trying to stop the pounding when I realized there was a pounding on the door as well. I cleared my head, got up from the floor, and answered the door.

"Are you all right in there, man?" It was the apartment manager.

"I'm OK," I answered. I stumbled to the door, fumbled with the lock, and hid my eyes from sunshine when I opened it.

"Did you hear anything from the Veterans Administration yet?"

"No, I'm still waiting."

"The building owner is getting angry about the rent. I told him that you were still waiting. The American Legion only paid two weeks rent. They really mess over Black people. If you were a white veteran, they would have paid the rent until your disability checks started."

"The way my luck has been, I don't have any reason to believe I will get any help from the Veterans Administration."

"You got letters from President Carter himself. I'm sure they won't put you out on the streets. You are a Vietnam Veteran. The Veterans Administration will come through. Watch and see."

"Thanks for the optimism. As soon as I get the rent, I'll be sure to let you know. If nothing happens, don't feel guilty about doing what you have to do."

"If I can help out in any way let me know, man. Where is your wife?"

"She's gone."

That's a shame, man," he said, shaking his head.

The man felt sorry for me, I thought. It was amazing how reality had changed. In Detroit, the guys envied my life style, here people actually felt sorry for me. I did not have time to feel sorry for myself, though. If I was going to eat that day, I thought, I had better start finding some cans.

I could take some of the pressure off my foot by leaning on the grocery cart I was pushing. The pain never stopped. I had to decide to either deal with the pain of walking or deal with hunger. The desire to deal with the hunger always won out.

As I picked up the cans to feed myself, I could not help but think of the years I had spent working. It was very hard to accept the fact that seven years with Chrysler, nearly five years with the Federal Government, and becoming disabled while serving in the Marines had all come to nothing. A few months before, I had been planning my retirement from Chrysler. Now, I was living in an apartment with no lights, gas, or furniture. I was also facing the dreaded fact that, soon, I would have to face living on the streets.

Each day seemed longer and longer, but in the end,

time seemed to pass too quickly. The apartment manager made his last trip to my door. He came early that morning. "You had better get out of here," he said. "The sheriffs are on the way.

"I'm ready," I said.

"Where you going?

"I don't now. I am still expecting some news from the Veterans Administration, though. Could I get you to hold my mail for me? I will come by from time to time to check."

"I'd be glad to do it, man. I just wish there was something more I could do."

"You've done enough, man. Things happen like they happen. Thanks man." We shook hands, and he left.

The sheriffs were coming up the stairs as the manager was leaving. I was ready to leave. I grabbed the back pack I had in the middle of the floor and headed for the door. There were no words exchanged. I walked out of the door and down the stairs. For the first time in my life I had no plan and nowhere to go. My future would be based on the biggest decision I had to make at that time. I stood on the street in front of the apartment, wondering whether to go to the right or to the left. I felt like I had been kicked out of the human race.

I turned to the right. Jackie Robinson Park was not too far away. I had enough gas in my car to get there, but that was as far as I could make it. I lay there in my car for days, not eating and hoping I would die and get it over with.

As the days passed, I learned to use the restrooms in the park to keep myself clean. I watched the children go to and from Dorsey High School. I began to be known as "the man who lives in the park." The men who worked in park got to know me; they would come up to the car to speak when they arrived for work. I soon found out that starving was not a good way to go.

I had never been out of work, so I knew nothing about food stamps or welfare. My first experience with unemployment benefits had turned out to be a nightmare. I decided to find a police station to inquire about getting help. There was one officer at the desk when I walked in. I explained to the officer that I was homeless and on the verge of starving to death. I asked where I could go to get some help or what could I do. The officer pulled his weapon, pointed it at me, and said, "I'd advise you not to break the law." I found myself laughing.

I began picking up cans again. I lived off cans of beans and bread, sometimes a package of lunch meat. I was seated in the park eating one day when Kool showed up. He was with another man dressed in a suit.

"Hey, man," he yelled. "What are you doing over here?"

"I live here."

"I came by your place a few times before I found out that they had put you out. I've been seeing you around picking up cans."

"That's how I'm eating these days."

"This is my friend Aamez. Aamez meet Twenty-five." Aamez was laughing mockingly as we shook hands. "Aamez lives in the valley. I have been slinging dope for him since Omar and Kojac started tripping on me. He deals dope like Omar and Kojac, the only thing is they operate on a bigger scale. These guys are more sophisticated than Omar and Kojac; they go to school and most of the customers are White."

"Why don't you sell dope, man, or steal or something. It looks bad, you picking up cans like that. Would you pick up cans, Kool?"

"Hell no! I would rob a bank and go to jail first."

"Selling dope and stealing its bad karma," said.

"Well here's another can," he said, as he walked to a can and kicked it towards me. He and Aamez were laughing uncontrollably.

"Don't do that," I said, walking towards Kool, preparing to knock his teeth out. "Uh oh," Aamez said. "He is getting angry. We had better leave." They were about to walk away when the three of us noticed a car speeding into the parking lot. Three men jumped out, running towards us. I backed away when I saw guns in their hands. Kool and Aamez both pulled guns as they turned and ran. The men fired at them, they fired back as they ran. For a minute, the place sounded like a war zone, then Kool and Aamez seemed to vanish into thin air.

I thought about the incident when I retired into my car to sleep that night. California was like the Twilight Zone to me. The thought that I had come there to die occupied my mind again.

I spent long nights in my car trying to come up with the one event in my life that caused me to end up here. I had never done anything but work and practice martial arts. That was before I started going to the bars. It felt like I had no life until I started dating the dancers back in Detroit. As I thought about how it all began, I realized that one very important decision may have led me to what I thought was my rapidly approaching death.

Racism was a big factor. I had been discharged from the Marine Corps for Physical Disability. I had been due compensation by law. However, the White employees at the Veterans Administration in Alabama had no problem telling me, "We ain't giving no nigger no compensation."

I was working at the regional office when a Black calmly approached me to ask where the contact office was. He smiled after I showed him the way. He held up a paper bag and told me he had a surprise for them. It was later that day that I heard the man had gone into the office and pulled a gun. He said that he and his family were starving, and the Veteran Administration was denying his benefits. The story was on the news and the man got a lot of years in prison. The incident taught me to never try to deal with the government with anger. I began writing the President presenting the facts.

I had not felt the effects of racism since I left Alabama. I made more money in Detroit than I had ever dreamed I'd make, and living good had made me forget. I had forgotten about the civil rights struggle that I grew up in. I had become completely engrossed in making money and partying. Dating the dancers was all I wanted to do.

I loved the fact that women thought I was cute; fun and sex was all that was on my mind. I was too playful and I never took anything seriously. I was having something like an affair with my supervisor Lois at the Veterans Administration in Detroit. However, I never took Lois seriously because I could not see her taking me seriously. She was too fine, to classy, and too intelligent. All during the relationship I wondered why she liked me and how long it would take her to get tired of me.

I know that I did not know the meaning of real love until I met Carrie Gaites. Carrie was not the most beautiful woman I had met. She was really cute and, to me, she was the sexiest. Her body was slim and athletic, her hair was jet-black with big curls, and I could not help but stare at her every time I thought she was not looking. She had been a track star in high school. She had a girlish laugh and beautiful pearly white teeth. I had too much respect for Carrie to hit on her. I respected the fact that she had a husband; she respected the fact that Liz and I lived together.

Liz and I lived one black away from Carrie and her husband. We both lived in Highland Park, Michigan. Carrie and I met each morning at the bus stop. We rode the bus to the Veteran's Administration Regional Office in Detroit. We worked on the same floor.

When Carrie sat next to me on the bus, my normal thinking pattern was thrown off. It was hard for me to contain my anxiety. She would place her hand on my knee and smile as we talked about a television program we had seen, a movie, or a sports event. All I could do was try to as hard as I could not to stare at her, while briefly stealing a glance every once in a while. With each glance I would think that God had truly made an angel when he made her. I felt blessed because she liked me and felt comfortable talking to me. I felt like her husband was one lucky guy.

It was very hard for me to understand the reasoning behind the signs of abuse I began to see on Carrie. There came a time when she began trying to hide black eyes and bruises. When she began trying to have serious conversations with me about our family lives, I always changed the subject because I felt that what went on in her husband's house was his business. My first encounter with abuse was seeing my stepfather abuse my mother. Personal experiences of abuse while I was growing up had traumatized me to the point where I never discussed the matter. I was too dumb to realize that Carrie's husband had began suspecting that she and I were having an affair.

I could no longer keep changing the subject, after she made the statement, "If I mention your name in any way, he gets angry." I was so nervous, I began sweating. "But I don't understand," I said. "We only ride the bus to and from work together. Other than working together, we never see each other . . . Why would he think we were having an affair?"

"He has been insanely jealous ever since we started going together. I don't know why I married him."

"Carrie, listen to me, you have to do something. I watched my mother go through that for too long. You're just too beautiful to have your body damaged like that."

"I've been thinking about moving . . . to Atlanta."

"Oh No! You're thinking about leaving?"

Carrie looked deep into my eyes. Out of shyness, I dropped my head. "Percy," she said. "We need to talk. I know you and Lois have a thing, but there are some things you should know."

"You can call me at home," I said. "Liz went to Alabama again. She has been complaining that I work too much and never spend any time with her. She says she wants to be with her family and friends for a while. I don't know when she's coming back."

"I'll call when I can," she said, as we stepped from the bus and joined the people rushing to punch the time clock. I ran fast. I did not want to get lectured again by Lois.

I worked on a floor filled with filing cabinets and women. I was the only male file clerk. In Alabama only men held the job. Men in Detroit could choose factory work. The factories always paid more. I was waiting for a job opening.

Lois saw me running through the file cabinets, trying to get to my desk. "Percy!" she called out. The women on the floor began to look at me and tease, "Uh Oh, poor Percy's about to be spanked by his girlfriend." They were teasing and laughing as I slowly walked to Lois's desk.

"What's the matter with you? You know better than to run in here," she said.

"Give me a break, Lois, I was just trying to get here on time."

"Yeah, Percy, but Clarence talked to me again yesterday about you and . . . did you wash your face this morning?" she said, taking my face in her hands and examining it like a mother would do to a child. I jerked my head away. I could feel the eyes of the girls peeking at me and laughing. "Stop embarrassing me, Lois . . ." I said. "Yes, I washed my face this morning."

"Well, I see something . . . Go to the restroom and wash your face and come back."

"Aw, Lois . . . I said.

"I mean it, Percy . . . You come right back, I need to finish talking to you."

I walked slowly to the bathroom like a child. I washed my face with cold water. It calmed me. I was trying to think of something silly to say to Lois when I left the restroom. Lois was on the phone.

Frances, another file clerk, had just placed some files on Lois's desk. She was passing the restrooms returning to her desk. "Damn! You look good," I said. "Just shut up, Percy," she replied. "I know that you are all talk and no action."

"What do you mean?"

"You know what I mean. You always talk about what you want to do to me but when I give you the opportunity, you have somewhere to go."

"You mean the other day, when I had borrowed my uncle's car?"

"That's right. When you said you were leaving early, I got off early so that we could leave together. I was ready to hang out. You took me straight home, and I wasted a half-day."

"But you said you were not feeling well, and I thought you meant it."

"I said that so I could get Lois to let me take off, fool."

"I feel so stupid, Frances. I thought you were sick for real."

"You are stupid, Percy."

"I'll know better next time."

"Come here, Percy!!" Lois shouted. She lowered her voice when I got to the desk, but she was whispering angrily, and the girls were already giggling and joking about what was happening.

"I heard what you said to Frances, and I don't like it at all."

"How could you hear anything? You were talking on the phone. I was watching you the whole time."

"We will talk about this later. You really make me sick sometimes. Go back to work."

Incidents like that happened often at work. I loved the job. I even loved being teased about Lois. Carrie was always teasing me, along with the other girls. This time she did not say anything. She smiled when I passed her, but I could tell she was sad. On our bus ride home, she told me that she would drop by my apartment later that evening.

My brother Ace had come to visit from Alabama. He had fallen in love with Detroit and had decided to stay. He and I were drinking beer when Carrie came over. Ace was bragging about May, his new stripper girlfriend. He promised to introduce me to Apache, a stripper who had become famous in Detroit, and Canada. In addition, it was near my twenty-fifth birthday and I had celebrating on my mind.

Carrie came by to inform me that she was leaving her husband. She was taking the car and driving to Atlanta. She wanted me to go with her. If, for nothing else, to help her drive. Everything in me wanted to take that trip. It was the perfect opportunity to start a new life with the woman I knew I could love for the rest of my life. I told her that I could not go.

When Carrie walked out of the apartment, I knew that I would never see her again. I felt like a piece of my heart was being ripped from my chest. I told Ace that I loved her and deep inside, I felt like we would have made the perfect couple.

"Then, why didn't you go with her?" Ace asked.

"Because I'm a coward," I said. "Things are going too well for me right now. For the first time in my life, I'm able to save money. I want to be able to put my children through school; I don't want them to have to grow up like me. I'm afraid to make a change."

Ace went to the refrigerator, grabbed two beers, and threw me one. "Yeah man . . ." he said. "She is fine . . . But you talk about Carrie as if you love her more than you love Liz. And I know you are not going to leave Liz, she's your baby's mother."

"I got with Liz on a bet. When Liz started working for the Veteran's Administration Regional Office in Alabama, she was the finest thing in the building; all of the guys were trying to get with her. I was too shy to join the competition, so they got together and bet me $100.00 that I would not ask her to go out. I went into her office sweating like I don't know what, asked if I could take her to lunch, and she laughed at me. I ran out of there as fast as I could. I felt embarrassed every time I saw her after that. Then one day, I had to deliver some mail to her office. I quickly put it on her desk and was about to run out when she said, "I thought you said you were taking me to lunch?' "

Minnie and I were married, but we had separated at the time. Minnie's family had already moved to Detroit and she was preparing to join them.

Liz and I started dating. The first time we had sex, we stayed in bed for three whole days! We only got up to shower and eat. Everyone at work was teasing us when we returned to work. We continued to see each other. When I moved to Detroit, it was not hard for her to decide to move with me. I made it easy for her to continue seeing James Harris, her fiancé.

I was anxious to meet the stripper Ace had talked about on the night. I let Carrie go to Atlanta alone. I felt guilty at first, but a couple of beers and Ace's description of the dancers made me forget quickly. I had not been in a strip club since I was in the Marines. Ace and I covered a lot of them that night.

The bar where May and Apache danced would be our last stop that night. We started out early. We had visited several bars before midnight. Round midnight we were in Bruce's Lounge on Livernois Ave. A dancer called Gypsy came to wait on our table. Top me, she was gorgeous. She had breasts so large that, you could not help but stare at them. Ace was drunk. He always got into arguments or fights when he got drunk. He wanted someone to argue with.

"What is your name?"

"Gypsy."

"Gypsy? How the hell did you get a name like Gypsy? You ain't no damned gypsy."

"I'm sorry you don't like me, but what can I get you guys to drink?"

"I want a beer."

“I’ll just have a Coke,” I said.

“Could I see you guys’ ID?”

“What the hell do you need to see our fucking IDs for?”

“Look, guys, I’m not trying to give you a hard time. I have to see an ID. My job depends on it.”

“Well, I don’t need no damned ID. I know who I am.”

Ace was drunk enough to get the attention of the bouncers and some of the other waitresses. There was a crowd forming around our table.

“I’m not pulling out any ID either,” I said. “I’m twenty-five years old today and, the legal age for drinking is eighteen. I know I look older than eighteen.”

“If you don’t want to show your ID, you’ll have to go,” one of the bouncers said.

Ace and I stood up to fight. “Wait!” the owner yelled, rushing towards the table. “Aren’t you the karate instructor at grand master Shim’s school?”

“Yes,” I answered.

“My name is Ron,” he said, extending his hand. “I own the place. Gypsy didn’t mean any harm. They are required to ask for ID. I’m sorry for the disturbance. You guys stay and have a drink on the house.” He nodded to Gypsy. She went to get the beer and Coke.

“My name is Chris,” another waitress said. “If you don’t like her, I’m here for you. Did you say this is your twenty-fifth birthday?”

“Yes,” I answered.

“Well hello, Mr. Twenty-five.” Chris had two long braids like an Indian. She also wore an Indian headband and wore a dancing outfit that gave her the appearance of an Indian. Gypsy came back to the table. “I got this table, why don’t you move on and tend to your own business?”

Chris gave her a nasty look, called her a bitch, and

left. "Here is your Coke, Twenty-five," she said. "I hope you understand that I didn't mean any harm." I felt good. We stayed at Bruce's until it was time for our dates with May and Apache. Gypsy and Chris asked us to come back. Before we got outside the door, the two of them were in the dressing room cursing at each other and fighting. The men in the bar had taken their attention away from the stage and were listening to the fight.

Ace's girlfriend May was a beautiful girl. Apache on the other hand, was like someone out of an adventure novel. She was nearly forty years old but she had a mystical beauty. Beautiful dark eyes, hair that fell below her waist, and the perfect figure. I was enchanted from our first meeting.

Apache was a self-proclaimed nymphomaniac. After we got to know each other, she promised to teach me everything about sex. Liz had gone to Alabama for too long. She gave Apache and me nearly four months together. Liz came back home and Apache got angry because she could no longer come over whenever she wanted.

This must have been near the time James Harris was to be discharged from the Marines. Liz had not been back in Detroit too long before I came home from work one night to find everything in the apartment gone. I was angry at first, but I had money in the bank, good credit, and it was time to remodel anyway. I refurnished the apartment, turning it into a playboy's pad.

Gypsy became my best friend. I began dating Chris. Gypsy informed me that her name was Dee Dee. Gypsy was her stage name. I began calling her Dee Dee. I could not help liking Dee Dee. She was always introducing me to other dancers. It began to seem as if every time Dee Dee introduced me to a dancer, me and the dancer ended up sleeping together. I never tried to sleep with Dee Dee. I considered her my good luck charm. Ace informed me that Dee Dee was known to practice witchcraft. This made me somewhat afraid of her.

Dee Dee told me that she had indeed practiced witchcraft at one time. Then she began seeing the evil. She said that whenever she was alone she would turn, and the Devil would be standing there. Those sightings made her give up witchcraft.

That was the beginning, this was the ending. The Devil must have played a big part in my life, too, only there was nothing more for me to give up. I had reached my lowest point. All I had to lose now was the car in which I slept.

I could survive in the outdoors. I had been taught to do that in the Marine Corps. Privacy, however, was a thing of the past. The park came alive during the day, especially after the school term ended. There were dozens of children in the city's summer programs.

I was lying in the car daydreaming when one of the park's employees tapped on the window. "I don't mean to disturb you, man, but we have a children's program here. Each day the city sends lunches for the children. We always have too many lunches, and we end up throwing the extras away. I brought one over. Me and the guys want you to know that you are welcome to one every day."

"Thanks," I said. At that point, I could not remember when I had eaten anything but canned beans and bread. I had just been lying there watching my life play backwards like it was a movie.

It was embarrassing having people feel sorry for me. I could not stand that. I also could not tolerate people making fun of me, as Kool and Aamez had done. I remembered grand master Shim's advice. "Work out two hours every morning and two hours every might, you'll never be a loser." I got out of the car and began working out. I began stretching and practicing martial arts all day, every day.

My skills were impressive, from having trained seven years with grand master Shim. People began gathering to watch. Other men who took martial arts began hanging out with me. I picked up a few students who I trained for free. I had matches with guys who came to challenge me. A crowd began to gather every day, we had long philosophical discussions, and no one seemed to mind that I was homeless.

"It's a damned shame, man. I'm supposed to be looking for a job and I'm hanging out with you guys every day. My old lady would kill me if she found out," one of the men said. The crowds grew larger.

The summer programs ended then school was back in session. Groups of school kids from Dorsey began coming to watch the martial arts demonstrations. I began teaching some of the children. I had gotten used to living in the park. I could keep clean by using the park's bathroom facilities and I warmed myself each morning by working out. There was a trumpet player who also practiced there every day. I began to enjoy working out to his music. I remember thinking he was bound to be famous some day.

Kool had disappeared from the scene for a long time. He was selling drugs for Aamez while Kojac and Omar had the contract on him. Just like before he thought that he had been gone long enough for Omar and Kojac to forget. He had to take a chance coming back into the area.

It was dark and I was trying to sleep, but I could not ignore the sounds of a struggle outside my car. Someone was being badly beaten. I covered my ears, hoping the fight would move farther away from my car. Then I saw Kool's face being smashed against my window. He was then thrown to the ground and three men were viciously kicking him.

"Wait!" I said, I got out of the car. I was nervous, afraid, and I did not want to make the men angry.

"You had better go back to sleep, homeless dude," one of them said.

"I'm not trying to get into your business. It's just that I know him, and . . ."

"This fool is about to die. Don't you be foolish enough to die with him. Get back in the damned car!!"

The man rushed at me, attempting to push me back. I evaded him and pushed him to the side. He then tried to punch; I blocked and pushed him away again. The other two men then attacked me. I tried not to hurt them at first, but as they became more desperate, my kicks and punches began to connect. When I began knocking each man down every time they got up, they gave up and walked off. I helped Kool to his apartment.

Three
The Black Mafia

"Somebody better explain to me what happened. I just can't understand what you guys are trying to tell me, and the Bible says 'Of all thy getting, get understanding.' Again. Why is Kool still alive? And, why are the three of you sitting here looking like you have been bitch-slapped?" Kojac was doing the talking. Omar was shaking his head. Johnnie-Reb and two other men were sitting on the sofa with their heads down. All of them wearing bruises.

"The guy saved him."

"Who saved him? Jesus, was it Jesus?"

"The guy who lives in the park."

"What does he look like?"

"He has long hair, and he lives in the park. That's all we know."

"Long hair, Huh? So it is Jesus. Is that what you're trying to tell me?"

"He was just too good with that kung fu shit."

"They will come claiming to be the Divine One, and they will be false the prophets, the Bible says. If you guys ain't man enough to do the job, get some help. Go back to the park, and if this mysterious longhaired man is still there, all I want to hear is that you beat the living shit out of him. I want him dead, I want Kool dead. Please don't come back until they are dead! You hear me? I'm the only Divine One around here."

The three enforcers left the house. Kojac was no longer worried about Kool. I was now the man they were coming after. The same three men came back along with three others. It was still an easy fight. The years I had trained under grand master Shim paid off with interest.

With the report that six men had been beaten, Kojac became concerned. He contracted an assassin he had met in San Quentin. The man owed Kojac a favor. The man looked like a killer. I remember when he approached me in the park. I was sitting in the grass meditating. I could feel the atmosphere change.

"Are you the man called Twenty-five?" he asked, walking up to me.

"I am."

"I'm a friend of Kojac."

"I've been looking for you."

"Kojac said you were good at martial arts. He was right, you are a real martial artist. Any normal person would be nervous when a stranger approaches. You just sat there relaxed and unmoved. I'm impressed."

"Thanks for the complement, but I know why you are here. Let's get this thing over with. I'm tired."

"I consider myself a real martial artist, too. As such I'll give you the respect of a fair fight. We'll go it hand to hand . . ." He took off his coat, folded it and placed it carefully on the ground. "If I lose, you find Kojac for me, tell him we're even."

We gave each other time to stretch. Then the fight began. We both did kicking demonstrations before the real contact began. He was stronger than me, but I was faster. The fight went on for nearly five minutes. Then I began to catch him with every kick or punch. He gave up after I held back two blows that could have killed him. He bowed, thanked me for sparing his life, and left with the promise I would not have to worry about him coming back.

A lot of the guys who hung out with me during the summer were present the day Kojac came to the park. He ignored the traffic as he walked across the street. When he got within hearing distance of our group, he began doing kung fu forms as he walked towards us. You could hear a loud rush of wind from each movement. He began telling the name of each move as he did the forms. Everyone was impressed.

He walked straight up to me. "You must be Twenty-Five, the Divine One?" "My name is Twenty-Five, but Divine One might be taking it a little too far," I answered.

"My name is Kojac. I was sent here like John the Baptist. Just like John knew Jesus when he saw him. I know that you are the Divine One."

"Did you come here to fight?"

"No, fighting you is the last thing I want to do. I saw what you did to my men. I was just wondering what a man with your talents is doing living in the park."

"You know what they say. Things happen."

"Just like I thought, you don't even cuss, do you? Where are you from, Twenty-five?"

"I'm from Alabama originally. I lived in Detroit for the last few years."

"I'm from Mississippi myself. I knew you were from the south. Real men come from the south. We know what being a gentlemen means; we know what it means to be a man. They told me that you refuse to sell dope. I don't blame you for that. You should get yourself off the streets, though. It's not gentleman-like. I got some ideas, if you are willing to go along with them."

"What kind of ideas?"

"Since you are so good with that karate stuff, you can earn a living by fighting. I'll put up five thousand dollars. Guys who want to challenge you can pay a hundred dollars. As long as you win, you get fifty dollars, off the top. You lose, I lose five thousand, and you lose your life."

"I sparred nearly every day when I was training anyway. I don't mind."

"Good, I'll arrange everything. All you have to do is win. Another thing. Kool was renting a room to some guy named Nitro. I don't think he still lives there. If Nitro is gone, I'm sure Kool will rent the room to you. After all, you saved his life."

"Thanks, Kojac."

"No problem, Twenty-five." Kojac then turned to the guys watching.

"All of you punks," he said. "Go out and tell all you see. You have seen the Divine One, and the time is at hand." He turned and walked off.

Kool got the word that Kojac had suggested he rent me the room. Trying to get on Kojac's good side, Kool came to the park to talk to me. "I've been trying to get that nigger Nitro out of my house anyway. He never paid rent anyway. He got out of the hospital a few weeks ago after he tripped out on PCP. He owes me for dope and rent. I went to the Page Four to ask him about it and he clowned on me in front of everybody."

"You should have hit him."

"What, and get killed? You don't know Nitro. He's an ex-prizefighter and a bouncer. He gets practice beating people up every day."

"Fighting is not a talent we're born with; it's a skill

that can be learned. Martial arts teaches you to defend yourself against anyone."

"Don't believe what you see in the movies. I have fought a lot of martial artists. I have beaten a lot of them. I'm pretty good; I could probably beat you. I've seen your moves. My arms and legs are longer than yours. Nitro is different, he's twice my size."

"It would take you five years to be able to fight me," I said. Kool jumped up and walked close to the other men seated in the park.

"Did you hear what this nigger says? I don't believe this shit. He said it would take me five years to kick his ass."

"Don't get me wrong," I explained. "I said you would have to train for five years to give me a good fight. You will never kick my ass."

"OK, let's go right now."

I successfully blocked and countered everything Kool managed to throw, then I kicked him around a bit to the roar of the crowd. He soon acknowledge my skill and offered to pay me to teach him how to beat Nitro. I began teaching Kool how to fight. I explained that learning to fight is different from learning real martial arts. Learning martial arts was hard and it took years. Learning to fight took less time, but it was just as hard.

Kool had already developed a dislike for me, and my becoming his teacher did not help the matter. I would let him attack, then show him a countermove. He got knocked down a lot. "It's amazing how he's able to actually execute those moves," one of the park employees remarked, as he watched one of Kool's training sessions.

"I think niggers be doing a little too much execution," Kool replied sarcastically as he got up from the ground.

I was with Kool in his apartment when Nitro came

by. I sat and watched as Kool asked for his key and Nitro tried to hit him. Kool kept ducking, moving, and catching Nitro with solid, painful kicks. When Nitro realized he was defeated, he reached for the key and gave it to Kool.

"Twenty-five, you'd better stop teaching this nigger that shit. You are going to get him killed." He put his finger in Kool's face. "Let me tell you something, little nigger. Them little kicks you are doing ain't hurting me, you know I'll just give you the key and leave because I don't want to have to really hurt you."

Kool's whole spirit changed after he defeated Nitro. He had accomplished something he never thought he would be able to do. "It was a decent fight," I said.

"You had better be careful. I'm getting better and better every day. You may be next on the list. Here is your key," he said, throwing the key to me.

I was very thankful. I was living inside once again, I could lock myself inside away from the world and I could once again write to the President for help.

My early morning workouts in the park had become a habit. I would leave the apartment every day, headed for the park. There I earned my living by fighting. Guys began coming from all over to try to their skills. Eventually I lost count of the fights.

Kojac introduced me to Omar. Omar and Evelyn were very likeable people. Evelyn loved to cook. Kojac's wife Debra visited often. They began inviting me over for dinner on a regular basis. There were always pretty women at Omar's place. Omar was like a real godfather. It was amazing to see people coming to him with their problems. Sometimes I felt like I had somehow landed in the middle of a gangster movie, only everything was real.

Omar had sharks in a fish tank. The guys would get excited about feeding time. The women did not like it.

Sometimes a stranger would show up and you would hear a conversation like, "Omar, you and me were in Quentin together, man. We know how it is out there, man. I need some help, brother. Do you know what I mean, I need some help."

"Calm down," Omar would say. "I know a guy who has a little warehouse robbery set up. I'll talk to him and tell him to let you in on it, as a favor to me."

"Thanks, Omar. I owe you man."

When I got to know them, I found out that Omar and Kojac had other homes and women that they were supporting. They would sometimes stop by with money, food, drugs, or gifts of flowers and jewelry. Evelyn and I became friends.

Evelyn had a large collection of jewelry. She told me about the gifts Omar brought after he had been abusive. I suggested to Evelyn that she start taking martial arts lessons. That way she could defend herself from Omar's attacks. She agreed. I began coming by to give Evelyn her lessons three times a week. I began meeting other women who were interested in classes.

Things worked out OK with Kool. I only slept in the apartment. I got up early and headed for the park early each day. Aamez came by after I had moved in. He began to look through my things. He opened a jewelry box that Mary had given me as a gift.

"Don't touch that," I said.

"Don't worry, man, I'm just looking. Wow, you have some nice stuff. You know it looks like you were telling the truth when you said you were a player in Detroit."

"I'm going to ask you one more time to leave my things alone."

"Why are you always getting mad? I'm just looking," Aamez said, continuing to go through my jewelry box. I got up and walked towards Aamez. He placed his hand inside his coat.

"I don't like sissies like you," I said, walking up to Aamez. He backed up to the wall. "You always look for trouble, trying to prove you're tough. Then when trouble comes, all you know to do is to pull your guns." I slapped Aamez hard. He pulled the gun from his coat. I took it out of his hand and slapped him again. He slid down the wall and covered his face.

"Now you are lost. As bad as you are, you are about to piss on yourself because now you are about to be killed with your own gun."

"Don't kill him, Twenty-five!!!" Kool yelled. "He didn't mean anything. He was just playing."

I put his gun to his head. He was shaking uncontrollably. "Since I pay half the rent here, I expect some privacy. You can come to see Kool and go through his stuff anytime you want. Stay away from me, and my things. Do you understand?"

"Yes, yes, I understand."

I turned the gun around and handed it to Aamez. "Go find someone to play with." He scrambled out of the door. Kool went along.

Before the door could close, Kool grabbed Aamez by the back of his coat and jerked him back inside. He frantically told us to be quiet. We heard the footsteps of someone coming up the stairs. Kool ducked down and put his ear to the door. There were several knocks, then the person left.

"I thought you had worked things out with Kojac," I said. "I have," Kool replied, "that is somebody else." Kool and Aamez waited for the person to leave, then they left.

I looked at the jewelry box that Mary had bought for me. I sat on the floor, thinking about the life I had been robbed of. I thought about my children and our nieces and nephews. I was thinking how weird my life had become. My thoughts were interrupted when I heard the same footsteps coming to the door again. I got up to answer.

There was a well-dressed Black man at the door. He spoke with a Jamaican accent. "Good morning," he said. "I am the building owner. I am looking for Dwayne." "You mean Kool?" I said.

"Yes. Is he here?"

"No, he left a little while ago."

"Can you give him a message for me?"

"Sure, what's the message?"

"Tell him that the rent is now too far past due. I'll have to take some action."

"Wait a minute. I share this apartment with Kool, or Dwayne, whatever his name is. I pay half the rent. I don't want to get kicked out unexpectedly."

"I haven't gotten any rent for over six months. I haven't been able to get in touch with Dwayne for three months. I'm going to start eviction procedures."

"Look," I said. "I know you won't understand this, but I was homeless before I rented this place. It is not good being homeless. I'm a disabled veteran and I don't have any definite income right now, but I can pay you some rent and some of the back rent to keep the place."

"I don't mind renting the place to someone who will pay. I am not going to continue renting to Dwayne. I'll have the sheriff come up to change the locks. You can take the place after he's officially out. The apartment is yours as long as you pay the rent and keep him away from the place. I want it understood," he said emphatically. "Dwayne cannot live here."

Events took place just like the man said. The sheriffs

came, Kool was evicted, the locks were changed, and I had my own place once again.

Kool, on the other hand, could not get any drugs to sell. Blue had become more involved with the decision-making. He advised Omar and Kojac not to give Kool any more drugs to sell. The organization was growing, and Kool could not be trusted.

It did not take Kool long to get into trouble with Aamez. This time, he was more down on his luck than he had ever been. He approached me about letting him sneak in to the apartment to sleep and shower. I told him that breaking my agreement with the owner would mean, I would get kicked out. I was not willing to take the chance. Before long, Kool was sleeping in the park.

Four
The Hit

"That's a cop," Blue said. "You guys are stupid. I'm not going anywhere near him. When you guys go back to prison, I'm going to be laughing."

"Twenty-five ain't no cop," Omar said. "He gets high too much. Cops can't do that. If you were a cop, would you take a chance smoking angel dust. You would be putting your life on the line. Hell, he lived in the park for months. Would a cop live in the park?"

"I've seen how good he is at karate. The only way you can get that good is to be trained by the government. Look at his car. Homeless people live in old cars. His car is pretty new. And look at the obvious. If I had those skills, I would just kick somebody in the head and take their money. Wouldn't you? Mark my word. Twenty five is a cop."

Everyone in the room was silent for a while. Kojac spoke out. "Twenty-five ain't no cop."

"Well, just do me one favor, let's investigate before we let him know too much of our business."

"It wouldn't hurt," Omar said. "It's always better to play it safe. He is a rather strange guy."

"He's the Divine One," Kojac said. "I keep telling you guys. You are just non-believers."

"He's the Divine Cop!" Blue said. "The reason he can smoke angel dust and still function is because he don't really smoke it. Don't you see, mark my words, I know a cop when I see one. Think about this, how many homeless people get letters from the Office of the President?"

With my own place, I spent more time at home. Sometimes I even dressed the way I did back in Detroit. No matter how, things changed for the better. I always ended up thinking about Mary. Omar sensed my sadness. "I know what you're thinking, little brother," he would say. "Go on; use one of the phones in the bedroom. See if you can get in touch with your wife."

Since no one but Kool had ever met Mary, the only thing they knew about her was what I had told them. When I mentioned that she had worked at the Page Four Lounge, Kojac questioned Nitro about her. Nitro had remembered her. "Yeah, I know Mary," he said. "She is light-skinned and talks real cool. She is from Detroit."

Nitro said that Mary had quit working some time ago. He promised to keep asking around.

There were so many fine women claiming to be Omar's sisters and cousins that I never knew if they were telling the truth. I was at the apartment one night when Omar got a distress call from Wesley. She was leaving her husband. She had rented a cheap motel room in downtown Los Angeles. She was afraid and wanted to come to his place to stay for a few days.

I was asked to go down town to pick her up. I was parked in front of the motel waiting when the police pulled up behind me. "What are you doing here?" they asked. "Don't you know that this is a no-parking zone?"

"I'm just waiting for a lady," I replied.

"Oh, so you're pimping ladies down here?"

"No, I'm doing a friend a favor. I'm not a pimp."

Wesley came out with her bags. I gave a sigh of relief and helped her into the car.

Inside the car, I felt like an idiot. Wesley was an aerobics instructor. She was over six feet tall and had a body that took my breath away. I found it hard to hold a conversation at first, but she was friendly. I was totally at ease by the time we got back to Omar's.

I began going to see Wesley; she began coming to see me. Soon we had an affair. We both had spouses that we had to make decisions about.

I was still faced with challenges in the park. Things were changing, though. The police had begun coming by when the crowds got large. With the police breaking them up, there were fewer matches.

One day I was approached by the director of the park. He introduced himself and told me that he had witnessed a lot of good fights and had spent sometime watching me work out. He felt that martial arts would be a good thing to teach the children. He asked if I was interested in teaching in a building in the park. I accepted.

When we talked about pay, he asked if I wanted to apply to work for the city. I told the director that the government had begun taking my paychecks and I could not be sure if they were going to continue to do it. Working for the city might not be a good idea. The director allowed me to teach in one of the park's buildings and to collect the fees as my salary. The classes were advertised in the community newspaper.

Kool was now experiencing what it was like living in the park. Knowing that I occupied what used to be his apartment made his hatred for me grow. He came one day to challenge me to a match. I beat him easily. He promised to go away to train, then come back for a rematch.

Kook knew my schedule. He decided to break into the apartment while I was in the park. I noticed that the apartment had been broken into, but I could not find anything missing. Kool had searched through my things and found a card from the Los Angles Police Department. The card read, "Congratulations, you have passed the written portion of the Police Examination." Kool immediately took the card to Blue. For Blue, this was the proof he needed to show that he was right about me being a cop.

The morning after my apartment had been broken into, I got into my car to find out that someone had broken into it as well. They had tried to remove the tape player but had not finished. There were screws on the floor where the thief had been working.

I mentioned the break-ins to Kojac. "Why don't you come over to Omar's about noon tomorrow," he said. "We'll find out what's going on."

When I got to Omar's place, there were a lot of people and a lot of sadness in the air. "What's that matter with everyone?" I asked. The men began shaking their heads. No one spoke for a while, then Omar said. "Kojac raped Debra."

"Wait," I said. "Isn't Debra his wife?"

"Yes, Marie, Wesley, and some of the other girls went to his apartment to see about her. He left her tied to the bed and bleeding from the anus."

"Kojac is crazy," one of the men said. "He is too used to be in San Quentin. His mind ain't right for the outside."

The men in the apartment all worked for Omar and Kojac. Everything got quiet when we heard people coming up the steps. There were five young men coming into the apartment followed by Kojac. Everyone greeted Kojac as if nothing had happened.

"You guys have a seat," Kojac said. There was fear in the men who accompanied him. Kojac stood in front of them and pointed his finger at them. "Last night, someone broke into Twenty-five's car. We know who the men are who are stealing these tape players. Now, let it be known that if my car, Twenty-five's car, Omar's car, or a car owned by anyone in this room is touched, we are going to kill all of you. You guys catch my drift?"

The men all agreed, and left the apartment in a hurry. To the men who remained, he said, "This is Twenty-five. He's one of us now. From now on, in this organization, his word is law. The chain of command is this: Omar, me, then Twenty-five. Twenty-five is third in command, everyone got that?"

"Twenty-five, that's a name? What is your last name then?" one of them asked.

"Five, fool!!" another one answered. Everyone laughed.

"Twenty-five," Kojac said. "We have an organization here. A tightly knit organization. We are going to take over the drugs, prostitution, a little of everything. We welcome you into our organization."

"No offense," I said, "but I don't do crime. It's bad karma. Everyone laughed again.

"You don't have to do anything that you don't want to do. Mainly, we all just look out for each other. That is all we really expect, that we get each other's back when the going gets rough. The way you fight, you don't have to rob or sell drugs; if you just watch my back I'll be happy."

A young man came running to the door. He rushed in and whispered something to Kojac. Kojac whispered something back, and the man ran back out of the door. "There is a white man in the Jungle flashing a ton of money. Two of you guys go and take care of that."

Two of the men got up and ran out of the apartment. Kojac resumed his conversation. "We are going into something that is going to make all of us rich. The new thing on the street is called Sherm. It's a Sherman cigarette dipped in PCP. They sell like mad. We are trying hard to find out how to make the stuff, but in the mean time, we got some pretty reliable people to buy it from."

"They say that Sherm is worse than angel dust. A lot of people die from using it."

"They will die no matter who sells it to them. The Bible says, 'those who will die, shall die.' In the meantime, let the dead bury the dead. Let us make some money."

"I got something I want to get cleared up," Omar said in a serious tone. "Twenty-five, you have been teaching these women karate. I don't think that is right."

Kojac agreed. "That's right, Twenty-five, these women don't need to know that stuff. Pretty soon they'll be using it on us."

"Martial arts is what I do," I said. "If someone asks me to teach them, usually I will. You guys will have to get that straight with your women."

"Let me put it this way" Omar said. "You can teach it if you want, if my woman uses it on me, I'm coming to get you."

"All I can tell you is, if you come, don't miss—because I won't." We stood there looking each other in the eyes. Omar walked away shaking his head. "This dude is crazy, man."

"That is why I made him one of us," Kojac said. "You guys see what I'm talking about? No fear, the Divine One has no fear."

The men who left earlier came back breathless and happy. They handed Kojac some stacks of money. Kojac quickly placed the money in equal stacks; he threw each of us one of them. I jumped when he threw one to me.

"I don't want that," I said. "Did you guys just rob somebody? Did you kill him?"

"Nobody killed anybody," Kojac said, laughing. They all began cracking up.

"And you guys call me crazy?" I asked. "I feel like I'm in one of those Western movies where, a man comes from the civilized east to the Wild West. You guys are crazy." I walked out of the door. Blue and three of his women were coming to see Omar and Kojac. When he saw me, he and the women turned and went the other way. I smelled trouble.

I went to the apartment and worked out well into the night. It was hard for me to relax. I could sense something about to happen. It was very late when there was a knock on the door. "Who's there?"

"Harriet."

I opened the door. "Hello, Harriet." She gave the smile of approval that women give men when they like the way they look. "Can I help you?"

"Where's Kool?"

"Oh, you're Kool's girlfriend. I'm sorry, Kool no longer lives here."

"Girlfriend? She asked laughing.

"Yes, he said he had a girlfriend named Harriet who lives in this building."

"Well I can assure you I'm not Kool's girlfriend."

"I'm sorry. My name is Twenty-five."

"Oh, you're the karate man."

"I guess."

"I was looking for Kool so that I could get some Sherm. Do you know where I can get some?"

"Omar probably has some, I don't sell it."

"Do you get high?"

"Yes."

"When I find some, I'll come up and we can get high together. Kool told me a lot about you."

“I’ll be looking forward to it.”

After Harriet left, I tried to meditate. I could not shake the feeling of uneasiness. I was thinking that maybe this was my night to die, then came the knock at the door.

“Come in,” I yelled. Kojac opened the door and slowly walked in. “What’s going on, Twenty-five?”

“What’s happening with you?”

“Nothing. Look, why don’t you come with me, let’s go get something to eat.”

“I’m not hungry.”

“Come on, let’s walk over to Omar’s. We want to take you out to dinner.”

“You seem nervous, Kojac. It’s not like you. I know what you came here for, it’s your lucky night. If you got to shoot, get it over with. I could have killed you when you walked in the door, I just don’t want to go to jail, and I’m tired of fighting.”

“It’s just like they say, you’re the bravest little nigger I ever seen too. And you ain’t no cop, are you?”

“Hell, no, I ain’t no cop.”

“That is what this thing is all about, Twenty-five. Blue thinks you are a cop. Kool broke into your apartment and found some card from the Los Angeles Police Department. The card said you passed the test to be a cop, now everyone knows.”

“I did pass the written part of the test. I failed the oral test. If I had a job, any kind of job, I sure wouldn’t be living here in the Jungle, hanging out with you criminals.”

Kojac laughed, “I told that fool you were no cop. I had better straighten this thing out with Blue and the boys. I should have known that anything from Kool needs to be checked out. You get a good night's sleep, Twenty-five; I'm going to find me a woman."

After that night, I found myself with two new friends, Harriet and Blue. Blue was a pimp who surrounded himself with gorgeous women. His apartment was in the same building as Omar's. There was always a gay musclebound bodyguard walking behind him. There was always at least two beautiful girls on each arm. Blue apologized to me for his thinking that I was a cop. He planned a party in my honor as a peace offering. Kool was ordered to stay out of the Jungle.

Kool became obsessed with taking revenge on me, Kojac, and Omar. After several weeks had passed, he showed up at my apartment to again challenge me to a fight. I beat him easily again. He ventured into Compton to find some fighters who were tough enough to beat Kojac and me and brave enough to bring a gang fight to the Jungle. The men showed up at Blue's party, intending to turn it out.

Our gang's security warned us the minute the men entered the Jungle. Kojac and me stood side by side in the center of the swimming pool that had been cemented over. As soon as the men entered the apartment complex, they charged. The balcony was filled with people from the party. There were at least ten men that Kojac and I fought that night. Omar's next door neighbor Glenda was yelling with the excitement of someone watching a professional sports event.

The fight went on for nearly ten minutes. Four of the men from Compton lay on the ground unconscious when someone yelled, "Police!" Everyone disappeared, except me and Kojac and the four unconscious men lying on the ground. A gang of policemen walked slowly into the pool area with their guns drawn. Kojac and I stood side by side in the same spot where we had met the gang from Compton.

"We heard there was a fight going on in here," one of the officers said.

"There was," I said.

"We heard there were guns."

"This is man to man," Kojac said. "No guns."

"What about them?" the officer said, pointing to the men laying on the ground.

"A little too much to drink, Kojac said. "They'll be all right."

"Well, if there are no guns, you gentlemen have a good night." The policemen walked backwards out of the area.

"What just happened?" I asked. "If we had been in Detroit, we'd be going to jail."

"There's a 'Mutual Combat' law here in Los Angeles; you can fight man to man as much as you want. The cops won't get involved unless someone pulls a gun."

Kojac and I turned to see Glenda looking down at us from the balcony. "I've never seen anything like that," she said. "I like what I saw here tonight. I really like it. Twenty-five, why don't you come up for a drink some time?" People from the party began coming up to shake our hands and pat us on the back.

Harriet was there. She put both arms around my neck in a sexy way, told me she had some Sherm and asked me to go back to our apartment building to get high. We left together.

Sherm was the name given to a Sherman cigarette dipped in PCP. The mixture of the tobacco and the PCP produced a different high than angel dust. Sometimes the side effects were amazing. The drug was known to completely change personalities and sometimes even physical appearances. Harriet and I had stayed up late into the night talking and smoking. Suddenly and, without warning, everything about her changed. She left the room, returned in a different outfit, grabbed my hand and asked me to go with her.

We ended up in Thrifty's drug store on La Brea Avenue. I asked her what she wanted to buy. She began stuffing stuff into her coat. She acted like she was in a daze. She went from aisle and aisle stealing stuff. I was embarrassed. "Wait, Harriet," I said. "I'm not in shoplifting." She began laughing. "Let's go," she said, grabbing me by the hand. We both quickly walked from the store. I could not understand her not being seen. I was preparing to be stopped by security. "Did you get anything?" Harriet asked when we got outside.

"No! I told you I don't do shoplifting," I said. She laughed uncontrollably. "I like you," she said. "Let's go back to your place and have sex."

Harriet made frequent visits after that night. I learned about her children's father. She said that he had gotten involved with some kind of drug deal in the Army. He was about to be discharged when he was arrested. He was serving time in a military prison. His sentence would be up soon. His dealings would have resulted in years of incarceration. However, there were some high-ranking officers involved, and some of the crimes were covered up to protect them.

Kojac continued looking for the recipe for PCP. In the meantime he continued to use the same suppliers. As sales increased, their price got higher. Kojac became angry. He asked me to ride along with him to have a business meeting with the suppliers. We drove to a place near Crenshaw Boulevard and Florence Avenue. The men inside looked tougher than the men who hung out at Omar's.

"So, what is the reason for the price increase this time?" Kojac asked.

"Cost of living, nigger," was the reply. "You guys are doing all right. We hear things."

"So you are raising the price because you hear we are making money?"

"I'm raising the price because I want to raise the price. Do you want the shit or not?"

"We'll take it this time. I'm just letting you know as soon as we find another supplier we're through doing business."

"You won't find a better deal, and soon you won't be able to find another supplier. We're expanding. We plan to be the major suppliers for this whole area. You deal with us or you don't deal."

"Me and Twenty-five don't want to hear about your dreams and ambitions. Give me the shit so we can get out of here."

"I wouldn't talk so tough if I were you. You forgot to bring back-up. Or are you guys strapped? You set out the money, then you'll get the shit."

Kojac reached inside his jacket and pulled out a stack of bills. There were four men in the room, and each man quickly pulled a gun as Kojac's hand moved.

"We never bring back-up or pistols when we're dealing with bitches. You can put your manhood away. We came here to do business, not to fight."

Kojac threw the money on the coffee table in front of the man doing most of talking. All the men replaced their weapons. One of the men got up and went into the next room. He returned with a brown grocery bag, neatly folded over from the top. The bag contained a glass quart-sized jar filled with PCP.

As the man handed the bag to Kojac, Kojac hit him hard enough to knock him against the wall. He never got back up. He kicked the coffee table over on the man sitting behind it, interrupting his reach for his weapon. I made a flying leap onto the two men seated on the couch as they reached for their weapons. The three of us turned the couch over. I quickly hit the one closest to me, then picked up a heavy glass ashtray and struck the other man in the forehead. The two men got up and ran from the apartment. Kojac had picked up the other man's gun and was now holding it to his head.

"Hey, hey, take it easy, Kojac. What are we doing here, man? We're friends, we both did time in Quentin together. What's this all about?"

Kojac never said a word; his hand slowly squeezed the trigger. I was terrified. "I'll tell you what," the man said sweating profusely. "Why don't you take this batch on the house." He reached own to the floor, picked up the money, and handed it to Kojac.

Kojac released the trigger and placed the gun in his belt, saying "Nice doing business with you, bitch!" I let out a loud sigh of relief when Kojac started for the door. "Let's get out of here, Twenty-five."

"Kojac, the next time you have something like that planned, please let me know. It was just luck that let me get to them two guys before they got the guns out."

"Wasn't no luck, they can't kill us. These punks coming along today have to have guns—without guns, they ain't men. Even with the guns, they are bitches when they come up against us, Twenty-five. If I thought they were capable of giving us any trouble, I would have prepared. When I say we are divine, I mean it."

On the way back to the Jungle, Kojac talked about how he had planned to take over the drugs, prostitution, and robbery operations. "We will have the workers selling dope on the streets and Blue's women can sell some too. They can do business in the nightclubs. Our organization will have to get stronger if we are going to have to deal with punks like the ones we just left. The next thing you know, they'll want us to work for them.

"We'll get some ledgers. We will keep the employee's names in one. Our business associates in the other."

"I wouldn't keep ledgers, Kojac," I said. "Ledgers are only evidence. You know everybody, and you know when someone is late with the payments. You don't need books. Keep the numbers in your head."

"You're right, Twenty-five: we would be collecting evidence on ourselves."

We both got nervous when a police car pulled up behind us. We were driving slow and the patrol car followed us for blocks. "We got a lot of shit in this car and this stuff carries a lot of time. We might have to fight our way out of this, Twenty-five. It's that or San Quentin."

Kojac pulled the gun from his belt and produced another one from beneath the seat. One he pushed towards me, the other he placed under his thigh. "Turn right," I said. "Let's see if they still follow us."

"No," Kojac said. "I'm going to turn left."

"You are already in the right lane, man. Make the next turn."

Just about that time, the lights and sirens came on. Kojac and I looked at each other as he pulled the car to the curb. The police car sped up, passed us and kept going.

"Man, that was scary," Kojac said. "We got enough shit in this car to get us fifty years in San Quentin at the very least."

"You'd be right at home."

"You'd fit right in yourself, Twenty-five. You don't know it but, you're just like us."

Wesley eventually went back to her husband. Harriet kept visiting. I found it amusing that she liked to talk about the Bible when she was high. I remember laughing when she told me how we would be allowed to smoke a little Sherm in Heaven.

Harriet bragged a lot about her children's father and the good times they had before he joined the Army. I bragged about Mary and the good times we had in Detroit.

My classes in the park went well. Johnnie-Reb became my star pupil and assistant student. We became well known and a lot of stories were spread about martial artists coming to the school to test their skills against us. Some of the stories were true, others were made up. Their made-up stories became more exciting.

Johnnie-Reb warned me about police beatings. He had started studying martial arts after he had been picked up and beaten by cops wearing Ku Klux Klan armbands. I had witnessed one of the beatings shortly after I moved to Los Angeles, during our stay at the Adams Motel. I walked outside one night and investigated some noises I heard in the alley. I saw several White policemen beating a skinny Black man. They were laughing and having fun. After the man was unconscious, a female cop placed her foot on the man's head as if she was posing for a picture. When I got close to the scene, the policemen pointed guns at me and told me to, "get the fuck out of here!"

The more time I spent at the school, the less I saw Omar and Kojac. Each time I did go by, there was another story about Kojac. Omar had enlisted the help of three

Hispanic men to help him do a robbery. They were waiting for Kojac to join them. One of the men was telling how Kojac had made him assistant in the robbery of a drug dealer. Kojac found the man in the bed with a woman. After taking all of the drugs and money, his accomplice was begging him to leave. Kojac decided to stay and rape the woman while the man watched, then he raped the man.

"Kojac stayed in prison too long," I said. "His mind is warped." "I don't think that's it," Omar replied. "Kojac was raping before he went to prison."

"Kojac raped him," one of the Hispanic men said, pointing to one of his companions. Omar and I looked at each other and shook our heads.

"Well, I've heard enough," I said. "I'm going back to the park to work out."

"Come over on the weekend, Twenty-five," Omar yelled as I walked down the stairs. "The girls are having a lingerie party."

I did return that Friday night and the lingerie party was hot. When I walked in, a well-built lady was modeling a silk outfit. I couldn't take my eyes off her. Evelyn was telling Omar and me that the party was for women only, we have to leave. The women were giggling; they didn't seem to mind our presence.

Omar and I were begging the women to let us stay when a young man came running to tell us that one of my students had broken his arm. We called an ambulance and followed the man through the alley where we met the injured child being helped back by some other boys.

I ran to the boy, picked him up, and was carrying him through the alley towards Omar's place. A crowd followed.

Through the noise I heard Harriet calling my name. I looked to see her coming towards us. She was accompanied by three men in military clothes. I suspected one of the men was Robert, her children's father. He was tall, good-looking, and well-built.

"I got to get to Omar's," I said, walking as fast as I could with the child. "An ambulance is coming."

Suddenly, the man slapped Harriet so hard that both feet left the ground. She fell hard. The man then picked her up by one arm and slapped her down again. "Get up!" he yelled. I could tell she was too embarrassed to cry. The three men looked at me and smiled as if the beating had taken place for my benefit. I hesitated for a second, and me and the men looked each other in the eyes. I looked at the child in my arms and hurried away.

I was back at Omar's the next day trying to get the woman's name who was modeling the black nightgown. Evelyn was teasing me about the women who had asked for my number. "Twenty-five, whatever you have that turns these women on like that, you should bottle it and sell it, boy. You'd be rich," she would say. "These women are crazy about you."

"I don't understand it, Evelyn. Why do women love gangsters?" I asked.

"It's different with you. You never let yourself get corrupt."

"Don't want to go to hell," I said.

Evelyn also informed me that Harriet's fiancé was in town. He was the man who had slapped her in the alley.

The more time I spent with my students, the less time I wanted to spend with my fellow gang members. I respected them as friends and brothers. However, I could not escape the fact that I thought they were a bad influence on my students. My visits grew less frequent, and I didn't care for them hanging around the classes. The whole situation was confusing for me. I had developed a great deal of respect for my fellow gang members, more respect than I had for those who considered themselves model citizens. At the same time, I did not want them around my students.

On my way to the laundry one day, I discovered the value of being connected. I walked out of my apartment with a pillow case filled with dirty clothes. I was waiting to cross the street when a police car pulled up in front of me. "What do you have in the bag?" one of the officers asked.

"Dirty clothes."

"What is your name?"

"Percy Brown."

"Do you have any ID?" I pulled out my wallet and presented my driver's license.

"Get in the car."

When I got inside the car, the two officers began laughing. "You're going for the ride of your life," one of them said. It was then I noticed the Ku Klux Klan arm bands on their arms.

They pulled off, but had not gone a block before Kojac pulled up in front of their car and blocked it. Kojac did not get out, but Johnnie-Reb came up in another car had parked beside the police car. He got out and walked over to the officers. Before he spoke, another car pulled up behind us and the police car was completely blocked in.

"Where are you taking our friend and why?" Johnnie-Reb asked the officers.

"This is a police matter, you guys had better move on."

"Bullshit! You can bet your White ass you're not taking him anywhere unless we know where he's going and why."

Both officers were sweating profusely. They were so nervous it was hard for me not to laugh.

"Look, it's nothing serious. We need to take him to the station to check something out."

"OK, you drive to the station. We'll be right behind you."

Both officers were dripping wet with sweat and could not talk without stuttering.

"Have you ever lived on the PCH?"

"I don't know what the PCH is."

"The Pacific Coast Highway."

"I'm from Detroit."

"This is just a little mix-up; we have a warrant for a man with the same name as you. His address is on the PCH, though. It's just an honest mistake, we apologize. We can't let you out on the street though; its against police policy, We'll just drive up to the station and you can leave as soon as we get there. I don't think you'll have to worry about a ride back." They pulled off with six cars filled with gang members following.

"Why did you pick me up?"

"You were coming out of the apartment with a laundry bag, and we thought you were a burglar."

The police car pulled up in back of a police station, I got out of their car and into Johnnie-Reb's car. The two officers rushed inside.

I visited Omar one day to find a White man in the apartment. They tried to introduce me to him, but I ignored them and walked straight back into the kitchen. "I need to see Evelyn, Omar. Do you mind?"

"No, little brother. Go right ahead," Omar answered. He got up and followed me. "What's up, Twenty-five? Why did you treat the man so cold?"

"A White man came to my place in Detroit one day,

asking me about joining the police. My life has never been the same. I prefer to stay from around White people."

"Give the man a chance, Twenty-five. Give the man a chance."

"Let me put it to you this way, Omar," I said, pointing my finger at him, "I don't do business with White people."

Evelyn was standing there watching Omar and me as our voices got louder. "Why don't you guys calm down? All this just ain't necessary. Richard is all right. Twenty-five. He's a friend of mine," she said.

Omar came close to me and whispered, "This dude Richard is going to show us how to make the PCP. Me and Kojac have been looking for somebody who knows how to make that stuff for a long time, man. This is money, Twenty-five, a lot of money."

I took a deep breath to calm myself before I spoke again. "Bad karma," I said. "But I'm a martial artist, not a drug dealer. That's you guys' business. From now on, I'm going to concentrate on martial arts. Don't get me wrong, I appreciate you guys and everything you did for me. If you need me, I got your back and hope you got my back, but take a word of warning, good does not bring about more good, but evil always brings about more evil. White people are evil. You guys be careful." I turned and walked out.

Johnnie-Reb spent a lot of time working out with me. I did not see Omar for a long time. Harriet could not visit because her fiancé was home. Kojac showed up at the park from time to time to play basketball or to work out. We started regular Saturday morning games. Kojac and I were always on opposing teams.

Kojac believed in winning at all costs. He would knock an opposing player down before letting him shoot. He would laugh and call the player a punk if he called foul. Eventually the only way you could make a basket was to fight your way to the basket. The young men who came to use the court could only watch until we were finished. The game became too dangerous. Eventually, I was the only man in the game who had not spent time in San Quentin. The guys began to call our game "Kill Ball" instead of basketball.

After the games I would stretch or meditate. Kojac always had a group of young men around him. He told them about prison life. He said that he and his friends were members of the "Five-Hundred-Pound Club." The members had to be able to lift five hundred pounds of weights, otherwise they did not consider you a man. He said that in San Quentin you were not allowed in the gym unless you could lift five hundred pounds. All of the ex-cons there looked like contestants in a Mr. Universe contest. I felt honored when Kojac pointed me out as the toughest man he had ever met.

Richard spent a lot of time at Omar's apartment. Soon Omar and Evelyn drove by the park to show off a new car. I suppressed my anger when Evelyn told me that Richard had helped them get the car at an amazing discount. "I told you he was all right, Twenty-five."

They invited me to dinner. I accepted on the condition that Richard would not be there. The lady who had worn the black negligee was there. Her name was Bobbie. I was consumed with lust for her because I could not remove the sight of her in that negligee from my mind.

Bobbie had a live-in boyfriend. He was an entertainer who did road shows and she never knew when he would show up. As Bobbie and I got to know each other, she began talking about her boyfriend Herb as if she needed to release the hostility she had developed toward him.

Herb had his clothes stored in her closets. There was a car and an RV that belonged to Herb in Bobbie's garage. When Herb did show up, it was only to take whatever money she had.

"Why don't you get rid of him?" I asked. "He won't go," she would reply.

"Surely there are ways to get a person out of your house. You could call the police."

"You don't know Herb. He is a gangster, like Kojac and those guys. He has threatened to hurt me if I call the Police on him, and I've seen him hurt people before. He means business."

"That doesn't make any sense. No one is stupid enough to think they can control a person like that. He does it because he knows you'll let him."

"Why don't you pay Kojac or Omar to ask him to leave? That is if you really want him to go."

"They are all old friends. Herb is a member of the gang. He sometimes goes along on some of their jobs."

"Do you want me to ask him to leave?"

She laughed. "You don't know Herb. You would have to kill him or he'd kill you."

"You don't know men," I said. "Things change when they are dealing with other men."

Omar and Kojac laughed uncontrollably when they learned that I was going to confront Herb. "Listen, little brother," Omar said. "When you go, please come by to get a gun. Don't be a fool. You don't know Herb."

It seemed as if everyone knew Herb but me. He arrived, as everyone knew he would, the day Bobbie got a check. I came by to see Bobbie, when I found out that he was there. I was sitting on the couch in the living room when Herb came in from the back of the house. I could see why people feared him. He looked mean and he had the muscles of a Five-Hundred-Pound Club member.

"Who are you?" he said, storming in to the living room.

"My name is Twenty-five. I'm a friend of Bobbie's."

"Yeah, Twenty-five, I've heard about you. Listen, Twenty-five, this is my apartment, and Bobbie is my woman."

I looked at Bobbie seated in a chair across from me. I was afraid that her fear of Herb would make her change her mind about speaking against him.

"I thought you told me this was your place?" I said to her.

"This is my place," she replied.

I laughed. "You're a liar, Herb."

"Twenty-five, let me talk to you in the bedroom for a minute. Man to man."

We walked into a bedroom. I went in a few steps; Herb stayed by the door. He closed the door and pulled up his shirt to show a pistol stuck down in his belt.

"Let me explain to you again. Bobbie is my woman and this is my place. I don't appreciate you being here. Now you see what I got in my belt. Do I have to get nasty?"

"You keep saying 'my woman.' If you were saying 'my wife,' I could respect that. I don't know who you think you are, but I think you're a freeloader. You intimidate these women, You force your way in and frighten them into letting you stay. You take their money and you call yourself a man."

"I'm a man. Like I said, I'm a friend of Bobbie's, not a freeloader who is out to take what she has. You don't intimidate me. Now, she wants you to leave. She wants your clothes out of her house and your cars out of her garage. I suggest you do that by tomorrow morning. If you don't, I'll come back to see if you can use your gun as well as you can your mouth. Unless you want to try right now. If you're not ready to try right now, I suggest you move away from the door."

Herb nervously stepped away from the door without hesitation. I walked through the living room, kissed Bobbie on the cheek, and left.

The next morning, Herb and his things were gone. Omar and Kojac could not stop laughing and talking about what happened. Omar said that Herb had come by his apartment before he left. "That is the bravest little nigger I ever seen in my life," Herb had told Omar.

"When he left, I told him, Herb, go and tell everyone that you encounter that you have seen the Divine One and the time is at hand," Kojac joked.

I went back to my apartment to see a woman playing football with the boys. I was excited by her beauty and her athletic ability. She could outrun, out-throw, and out-catch all of the guys. I sat on the steps watching her. She realized I was interested. I was thinking of the best way to start a conversation with her.

A tall slim figure walked into the gate. It was Kool. He broke up the game. "We are going to need some room in this courtyard," he said. "There is going to be a fight, and someone is going to get hurt. Come on out, Twenty-five.

I laughed. "You think you're bad enough to call me out, Kool?"

"I found another teacher. Better than you. I've been practicing. Come on out!"

Once again I beat Kool easily. I, however, wanted to show off for the woman who was visiting. I deliberately let the fight go on longer than it should have so that I could demonstrate my skill.

Harriet, her fiancé, and his two military friends came outside to watch the fight. No one had seen Harriet outside since Robert had come home. She did not look happy. I was beginning to think she was being kept inside against her will.

Kool left a beaten man. The children were excited by the fight. "They could use you in the movies," one of the boys said. The three men in military clothing came up to me. "That's nothing," one of them said. "Whenever you're ready, we'll show you a real fight."

I smiled and bowed. "I'm not looking for a fight," I said.

The lady who I had been showing off for interrupted our conversation. "Excuse me," she said. "Do you have a minute?"

"Pardon me, gentlemen" I walked over to the lady. The three men backed away. Harriet ran into the apartment.

The lady who had attracted me was named Linda. She worked for Hughes Aircraft. She had also been a track star in school and she had a scrapbook filled with newspaper clippings about her victories. She was in the neighborhood visiting a friend. She mentioned she liked the neighborhood. She was considering moving here.

"You don't want to move into the Jungle," I told her as seriously as I could. "You have no idea what goes on around here. Take my advice, find another neighborhood."

"You live here," she smiled and said sarcastically.

Linda did not take my advice. She moved into the apartment building next to mine. She came to visit as soon as she moved in. I reminded her that I thought it was a bad idea to move there. I warned her to carry some type of protection. She learned what I was talking about on her first payday after she moved in. She was robbed on her way home from the bank.

I was telling her that she was lucky she got away with her life. She was angry. She did not want to admit that the Jungle was controlled by gangs. "The next time, I won't just give up my purse," she told me. "I'll make them fight for it."

"Wrong idea," I said. "These guys are ex-cons. A lot of them have been in prison most of their lives, lifting weights. You don't have a chance."

"You're the one who doesn't understand," she said. "You talk about the place, but you live here. Honest working people can't let these thugs intimidate them. You don't let them run you out, and I'm not going to let them run me out."

"Look, I'm kind of stuck here. I don't have any control over my destiny right now. You have a good job and a choice. Please get out before it's too late."

The next payday, Linda was again on her way home from the bank. A man came up to snatch her purse. Linda held on desperately. She wrapped her hands around the purse straps, determined not to let go of the purse. She was dragged down the street until the straps broke. She had injuries to the face and the whole right side of her body where she had been dragged along the concrete. She did not look the same when I visited her. She had been tough, but she had been broken physically and mentally. She decided to move out of the jungle.

I went to Omar and Kojac to talk about finding the men who had robbed Linda. They told me they were glad I had come over. They were about to go on a mission. They needed my help. I probably would have gone along with them, but there were several ladies in the apartment. Bobbie was one of them.

Omar, Kojac, and some other guys were talking about the job they were about to do. I pulled Bobbie to the side and talked to her about having sex. She agreed. I announced that Bobbie and I were about to leave. The women were giggling. Omar and Kojac were almost hysterical. "No, Twenty-five! Don't leave. We got so important business to attend to."

"I got some important business right here," I said. Bobbie and I went downstairs to her apartment. We had sex, I went to sleep. Late that night, Omar and Kojac came into Bobbie's apartment as happy as I had ever seen them. When Bobbie opened the door, they forced their way past her and in to the bedroom.

"What is going on?" I asked.

"We are partying, that's what is going on. All of us are about to be rich." Omar took out some bills and threw them on the bed. "Here, Twenty-five, here's your share."

"My share of what?"

"And here is a little something if you feel like getting high," Kojac said before Omar could answer. He threw a Sherm wrapped in foil on the bed. "Richard has shown us how to make our own PCP. We don't need them fools anymore, we're going to be rich."

"The White boy?" I asked.

"Yeah, we told you he was cool."

I unwrapped the Sherm, lit it, and took a hit. I think I experienced death. At first it felt like my being was being sucked away as if it were in a vacuum cleaner. I lapsed through some kind of tunnel and ended up in a field filled with beautiful green grass, flowers, and trees. The place looked as if it had never been touched by civilization.

I felt good. Better than I had ever felt before. Everywhere I turned there was beauty. I heard someone calling me from one of the trees. I walked up to it. There was a beautiful woman with long flowing hair sitting high up in the tree smiling. We just looked and smiled at each other. I felt like I never wanted to leave the place.

Then I heard another voice. This one sounded like it was crying. As the sound of the voice drew my attention, I began regaining consciousness in Bobbie's bedroom. I found myself completely nude with my hands and feet tied. Bobbie was crying, Evelyn was crying, Debra was there, Glenda was there, all the women from the apartment building, and nearly all of the women from the Jungle.

"What in the hell is going on!?" I yelled trying to cover myself, but finding my hands were tied behind my back. "He's alive!!" I heard one of the women yell. A bunch of women came to the bed trying to kiss me. I was going crazy trying to untie myself.

After I got dressed, they explained to me that I had lost consciousness as soon as I took a puff from the Sherm. When I began speaking unintelligibly, they all felt that I may hurt someone without realizing it. The guys tied me up. Debra, Evelyn, and Bobbie called their girlfriends to find out how to bring you down off that stuff. Most of the woman in the Jungle were in Bobbie's bedroom looking at my nude body. Now, I had to live with the fact that every woman in the Jungle had seen me naked.

I still had the Sherm that Kojac had given me. I looked at it when I got to my apartment. I thought about my experience. If I had actually died and gone to another world, I sure wanted to go back. This time my only worry was, would God consider it suicide if I died of a drug overdose? Was that place Heaven? If I smoked it again, would I end up in the same place or somewhere else? I was about to light up when the phone rang.

"Hello, Mr. Brown?"

"Yes."

"This is Mrs. Carter."

"Huh?"

"The President's wife."

"The first lady?"

"Yes, Mr. Brown, we want you to know that we are looking into your case with the Veterans Administration. Everything is going to be OK. Are you all right?"

"Yes, I'm fine, Mrs. Carter."

"Good-bye Mr. Brown."

I never had time to recover from the shock. Kojac and three other men were pounding on the door. "Twenty-five, open up man." I let them in.

"That stuff must be good," Kojac said. He was in an extremely good mood as he walked into the apartment. "I was telling these guys, if it will knock Twenty-five out, it'll knock anybody out."

"Don't you think the stuff is a little too potent to put on the streets?"

"Not at all, Twenty-five, the niggers are always complaining about the stuff being too weak. They want the bomb, we'll give them the bomb."

"You don't understand what happened to me when I smoked it. Don't put it on the streets, Kojac. A lot of people could get messed up with that stuff."

Kojac looked around at his companions and laughed. "You can't stop us today, Twenty-five, you can't even stand up straight. That's what the niggers want, that's what they'll get. I'm putting the stuff on the streets." They walked out.

I was angry. I became angrier after I tried to move around and found out that I did not have full control of my movements. I sat down in the meditation position, feeling helpless but only for a moment. The anger took over. I put on a jogging suit and left the apartment running as fast as I could. I ran down Coliseum Boulevard to La Brea Avenue, then up the hill that seemed to go up for miles. As the sweat began to pour, I began to feel sober. After about two hours of running, went home to shower. I dressed and went to Omar's to find Kojac.

"Where's Kojac?" I asked, walking in without knocking. Immediately I felt the tension inside the apartment. Johnnie-Reb was with Omar. They looked as if someone had died.

"I'm glad you showed up, Twenty-five," Johnnie-Reb said. "Omar is about to kill Kojac."

"What's going on?"

"Richard and Kojac cooked up some scheme to get ten thousand dollars from the bank. They came up with some phony ten thousand-dollar check, and talked Evelyn into trying to cash it. They locked Evelyn inside the bank and arrested her."

"Is she in jail now?"

"Yes, Twenty-five and I warned Kojac before they made the deal that, if Evelyn went to jail, I would kill him. I meant it."

"Slow down, Omar. You are going to ruin things for yourself. Evelyn is a grown woman; she knows what she's doing. The thing for you to do now is to get her out, not get arrested yourself. Don't send yourself to prison, Omar. There are always different ways to handle things."

Johnnie-Reb looked out the window to see Kojac walking up the steps. "Kojac is coming," he said excitedly.

"Put the gun away, Omar," I said. "Put it away."

Omar reluctantly put his gun under a newspaper on the bar. He stayed close to it.

"What's going on?" Kojac asked as he entered the apartment.

“Evelyn is in jail, Kojac. I told you that damned check thing wouldn’t work.”

“Don’t worry, Omar. Richard is arranging for her to be released right now.”

“That’s not the point, Kojac.”

“Come on, Omar. You and me have been working together too long to fall out over something like this. I came by to tell you how much money we’re making off the Sherms. We can’t get them on the streets fast enough.”

“I was looking for you to talk about that Kojac. I was telling you earlier the stuff is too strong to be put on the street. It’s going to kill people.”

“Come on, Twenty-five, did you think I wasn’t listening to you? We talked about it and we weakened it. I’m not out to kill anybody, Twenty-five. The stuff is selling faster than we can put it on the streets. I had to hire some more men. I ran into Kool. I let him have twenty-five of them, just to help him get back on his feet.”

“You actually gave dope to Kool? Knowing the problems you had with him in the past?”

“He came to me for help, Twenty-five; I gave him my word that I would help him. I’m trying to straighten my life out, to be less corrupt, like you, Twenty-five.” We all frowned.

“I’m not going to be happy until Evelyn is home, Kojac. I suggest you look into that before anything else.”

“I told you, Richard is taking care of that. Evelyn will be here in a couple of hours. In the meantime, I want to dip some of these Sherms. The workers are waiting.”

Kojac took some cartons of Sherman cigarettes out of a paper bag. He carefully took a jar of PCP out of his pockets. He sat down on the floor and began to dip one end of the cigarette into the jar then the other. He would then wrap the finished product in aluminum foil. This was the way Sherms were prepared. Kojac was over-anxious, the process was too slow.

"Forget this." He emptied some packets of Shemans on a long piece of foil. He then took the bottle of PCP and poured it over the cigarettes. "This is faster."

"That won't work." Omar, Johnnie-Reb, and I said it at the same time.

"They have to be dipped one at a time," Johnnie-Reb said.

"Do you think them stupid dope addicts will know the difference. Look at them, don't they look like they have been dipped? Come on, help me wrap these things in foil."

"I'm not touching them," I said. "I got a call from the First Lady, Mrs. Carter. There is a chance the Veterans Administration is going to pay me the disability they owe me. That means I may have a chance to get out of here and lead a normal life again. I'm not doing anything that might send me to prison."

"I'm not touching them, either," Johnnie-Reb said. "You're going to have every dope addict in the Jungle looking for you if you put them out like that."

"Look at this one, do you really think some stupid dope addict is going to recognize the difference? All they want to do is to get high."

Omar walked out of the room shaking his head. Kojac quickly wrapped a bunch of improperly processed Sherms and hurriedly got his equipment together. "I got to go and get this stuff to the pushers." He rushed out of the door.

Omar was still angry. "He's lucky you were here, Twenty-five. I would have killed him."

"It's just not worth it, Omar."

"Let me give you some advice, Twenty-five. I'm just telling you this because I love you like a brother. If you keep fooling around with that damned Kojac, you're going to end up dead or in prison. I'm serious, little brother."

"I hear you," I said as I walked out.

The call from Mrs. Carter gave me the hope that I could still get back and regain the life that I had lost. My life in California still seemed like a bad dream. If the Veterans Administration would pay me retroactively from the time I was disabled in the Marines, I would have enough money to move back to Detroit, possibly pay off the court, and be with my children again.

I did strenuous workouts to fight the anxiety I was feeling about leaving. I stopped getting high and the pain returned. I was determined to clean my life up so that I could make a new start.

Only a few days had passed when three men attacked me in the park. The men were weak drug addicts and I beat them easily. They ran before I could ask them the reason for the attack.

I was attacked a second time by another man before I walked from the park to my apartment. He came after me with a baseball bat. He missed a couple of swings and I knocked him out with a spinning heel kick. I revived him and tried to ask what was going on. He struggled to his feet and ran away.

After that fight, I walked to Kojac's apartment to find out what was happening.

I found Kojac seated alone in the dark. "Come on in, Twenty-five. I figured they would send you to do the job."

"What job?"

"Don't play dumb, Twenty-five. They sent you to kill me just like they once sent me to kill you."

I sat down on the floor and crossed my legs. "I didn't come here to kill anybody. I did come to ask why these addicts keep attacking me?"

“There is a hit out on me. I didn’t know it was out on you, too.”

“For what?”

“Those Sherms I put on the street were no good. All of the customers want my head on stake. I found out that Kool told everyone I deliberately tried to cheat them. He is supposed to be with those soldier boys now. I think this is it, Twenty-five.”

“I told you not to let Kool in on this, Kojac.”

“I know. I also know that I should have killed Kool a long time ago. I kept letting him get away.”

“You know what I think? I think Kool, you, me, and the others have all been sentenced to die. We all keep getting our sentences delayed, but, I’m beginning to think there is no way out. We are genocide victims.”

“I can remember when all I wanted was a decent job and a normal life. If you talk to the rest of the guys you’ll see, we all had those ideas at one time. We all found out that the system is stacked against us. We don’t get to decide who are the cops and who the robbers. We have already been chosen to be the bad guys, the gang members. The strong men do what they have to do, we end up in prison, and the weak go to work every day, and get drunk or high to avoid facing the reality of their miserable lives. They’ll get rid of you and me somehow. They don’t have choice; them baby boys like Kool will be all that’s left of our race. Punks who live by the gun because they know they can’t call themselves men without them.”

“I once read an Asian proverb that said, ‘A stupid man dies a stupid death.’ I don’t mind dying. In fact, I think I’ll be glad to get out of here. I just don’t want to die on their terms. If the addicts think we cheated them, we need to straighten it out. We can do that. I’ll get up whatever cash I got, and you do the same. We'll walk through the Jungle tonight.

"We'll locate as many customers as we can. We'll tell them that somehow a bad product got on the streets. We'll tell them that we are ready to refund any of their money or replace the product. If we reach enough of them, the word will spread on the streets. Them Special Forces guys are a different story. They have been wanting to fight since they got here. I say we find them before they find us."

"You know, Twenty-five, you changed my whole outlook." He jumped up from the floor. "Let's do this. Tonight we handle all unfinished business. Before we leave the building, I need to holler at my apartment manager. I believe he's been screwing my wife. I want to handle that before we leave."

Kojac and I walked out of his apartment and headed for the manager's apartment. There was loud music and the smell of marijuana coming from the apartment. Kojac knocked, the manager opened the door. There was the sound of a party going on inside.

The manager came, opened the door. Seeing Kojac, he came outside then closed the door. The size of this man was amazing; he actually made Kojac look small. "I left you a message to get in touch with me earlier. What the hell happened? Why are you coming just now?"

"Let me give you one of them San Quentin pep talks. I told you not to come to my house leaving any messages. You stay away from Debra. That ain't my girlfriend, that's my wife."

Kojac turned to walk away. The manager lunged forward to grab Kojac's shoulder. Anticipating the move, Kojac turned, blocked the man's arm, grabbed it with both hands, and broke it with his knee. The man screamed in pain and tried to punch with the other arm. Kojac took the other arm and broke it over his knee as well. He then took the bigger man and lifted him above his head. He walked to the edge of the balcony and threw the man from the second floor to the courtyard.

"I been wanting to do that for a long time, Twenty-five. Let's go."

We spent most of the night paying off PCP users. It didn't take long for the word to spread that we were offering refunds to make up for the bad dope. It was close to dawn when we went to Harriet's apartment. Harriet smiled when she saw me and Kojac standing at the door. Her fiancé was there without his friends.

Harriet invited us in. Her fiancé nervously looked around as if he were looking for a weapon. "Don't get excited, man," I said. "We didn't come here to fight."

"I don't know," he replied. "I see you brought your boy."

"Not to fight you. I heard you guys bought some bad Sherm. It came from us. We want to make it right by replacing the Sherm or refunding the money. We can pay the money now. Kojac will be replacing the dope tomorrow. Which one do you want?"

"Kool told us that you guys deliberately put bad dope on the streets. He said you tried to force him to sell the stuff. He was telling us how he threw it back in your faces."

"Kool has been here?"

"Yes," Harriet said excitedly. "He told us that when he found out what you guys were up to, he went back and threw the dope in your faces. You should have seen the act he put on."

"Do you know where Kool is now?"

"He's helping Robert's friend look for you two."

“Let’s go, Kojac.”

“I don’t have any way to contact my friends to let them know to stand down.”

“Don’t worry,” I said. “Fighting us won’t be like fighting women.”

Harriet smiled. Her fiancé dropped his head in shame.

We were on the way back to Kojac’s apartment when the two soldiers showed up. Kool was standing back, watching as the fight began. Both men were good, strong fighters. However, their skills were no match for mine and Kojac’s.

Realizing they could not win, the men drew concealed weapons. One of the men fired. A bullet grazed Kojac’s arm. I did a forward roll and ducked as the soldier fired at me. Kool threw the other soldier an Uzi. He fired into the air.

“All you have to do is breathe too loudly,” the soldiers said. “We’ll put more holes in you than Swiss cheese. You guys didn’t think you could beat Special Forces, did you?”

There was no way Kojac or I could get to them in time. We looked at each other.

“What do you think, Twenty-five?”

“I say we take it to the dirt, Kojac. I’m so tired of California. I don’t know what to do.” I smiled. “See you on the other side.” We nodded and prepared to make our move.

There was the sound of a lot of guns firing into the air. The soldiers looked around to see Omar and ten other gang members. All of them had guns aimed at the soldiers.

The soldiers nervously dropped their weapons, raised their hands, and slowly backed away. When they felt that they were at a safe distance, they turned and ran. Kool took off running in a other direction.

"Where is Kool?" Kojac asked.

"There he goes, running between those two buildings," someone answered.

"I'm going to kill him!" Kojac yelled, running toward Kool.

"No, I'll kill him," I said, running along with Kojac. As I was running, the words began to echo in my head, "I'll kill him. I'll kill him."

Then I had flashes of Kool sitting with me and Mary smoking weed. Then in my dark apartment eating stolen bread and smoking weed. I stopped running. All of my strength left. Suddenly, I did not want to fight anymore. I just wanted to go home.

I walked back to where Omar and the rest of the gang were. It wasn't long before Kojac joined us. Kool was used to running and hiding. He always got away. Something up there is looking out for him, I thought.

"I got some news for you, Twenty-Five," Omar said. "Somebody named Dee Dee called, she said she was your sister-in-law, and she wanted to tell you where you can locate your wife."

It was hard for me to contain my excitement. It finally looked like things were really changing for the better. Omar and I started walking toward his apartment. Kojac joined us.

"I'm going to need to pick up some more stuff to replace the dope I need to replace and to get our business rolling again," Kojac said, addressing Omar.

"I don't know where the stuff is. You and Richard were responsible for hiding it."

"It wasn't me and Richard, it was you and Richard."

"You're wrong, Kojac. Richard said you and him were going to put it in a safe place."

"Where is Richard?"

"I haven't seen him for a while."

"Omar, I know you're not going to tell me we lost eight gallons of shit. We're talking about big money now, millions."

"We had better talk to Blue, he knows what's going on, and he'd better."

We were near my apartment, so I said good-bye and walked away from the group. Kojac and Omar continued their conversation as I walked away. Later, Kojac came by my apartment. "It's fucked up Twenty-five. It's fucked up."

"What do you mean?"

"Richard showed us how to make PCP. Embalming fluid is one of the main ingredients. We had got hold of eight gallons of the stuff, now no one knows where it is."

"Embalming fluid? Is that the stuff I smoked that night when I ended up naked with all those women in the room?"

"That's what it was. Now no one seems to know where the eight gallons went. I had to give Omar one of them San Quentin pep talks. I told him, from now on, I want mine off the top."

"What are you going to do?"

"I still got dope to replace. I've got to do something, but I'm going to give you a little advice, Twenty-five. If you don't stay away from that damned Omar, you are going to end up dead or in prison."

A cold shiver ran down my spine as I recalled Omar saying the exact same words about Kojac.

Kojac did not have the funds to make another buy. He decided to do an early morning robbery to raise funds. He robbed a McDonalds on Crenshaw Blvd. The police got to the scene before he could get away. There was a long shoot out. The SWAT team was called. Kojac's car was so badly damaged by bullets that it was unrecognizable. The only other vehicle on the street was a garbage truck. Kojac made his way to the garbage truck. He shot the driver, took the truck, and made his getaway. Kojac's shot-up car made the morning news.

Mary was working in downtown Los Angeles. She had a job at the Transamerica building. I called and arranged a lunch date for the next day. I got some rest and cleaned myself up. Somehow I was beginning to think I was coming out of the nightmare that I thought would never end.

I felt like my old self as I left my apartment headed for the bus stop. Kojac was on his way to see me as I was leaving. We stopped to talk in the middle of Coliseum Blvd. Neither of us paid any attention to the passing traffic. "Twenty-five, come on and go with me, I need your help with something."

"I can't do it, Kojac. I just heard from my old lady; I'm going to meet her right now."

I could not help but notice that one of Kojac's forearms looked as if it had been hit by buckshots. "What happened to your arms?" I asked him.

"Oh, this is nothing; I was just doing a little work and got bruised. Look, Twenty-five, I just contacted some friends in Las Vegas. They got a sweet deal going down there. Me and you could fit right in; we'll be rich in no time. Together, we could take over."

"Can't do it, Kojac. I'm still hoping I can get back to working a nine to five, paying my bills, and playing with my children on the weekends."

"What are you going to do, Twenty-five?"

"First, I'm going to find out if my wife is all right, then I'm going to get myself off dope, and go back home to Alabama."

"Back to Alabama, huh?" Kojac smiled. "When you get to Alabama, you tell them the time is at hand." We hugged, then walked off in different directions.

There was something magical about my bus ride into downtown Los Angeles. It was like I was seeing L. A. for the first time. In some ways I felt like my old self, but deep inside I knew I was just not the same person. Because of my experiences in the Jungle, I knew first hand what it mean to be born again.

Five
The Birth of Crack

The number of pretty girls working in the Transamerica building was amazing. Whoever did the hiring was a person after my own heart. Mary looked right at home. She had changed as well. She had studied to get her GED and, had plans to go to college.

"Twenty-five, always thought that you would find me and save me," she said after we hugged.

"I found out that I couldn't even save myself."

Mary had taken an extra hour for lunch, so we had a long friendly talk. The fact that she was doing well took away my feelings of guilt. I always worried that, if anything happened to her, it would be my fault for bringing her to Los Angeles.

On my way back to the Jungle, I felt good. I even felt like the punishment for my sins was complete. If my monthly veterans compensation was enough for me to live on, I would have time to go back to school to work on a degree. I was also interested in finding another grand master to continue my training in marital arts. I still had classes going on in the park. However, I wanted to be a real master of marital arts and for that, I needed more training.

My use of PCP decreased after my out-of-body experience. I still found myself wanting to get high in order to deal with my physical pain. I began using mostly marijuana. Linda came by my apartment some nights, and some nights I spent at Bobbie's. No matter where I was, I had developed the habit of jogging early in the mornings. I was returning from a run one morning when I noticed the SWAT team moving in on Omar's apartment building.

I rushed over to Bobbie's to call Omar. I told him to get rid of his dope. The police were in the building. I took a bag of weed I had in Bobbie's bedroom and flushed it down the toilet. "What are you doing?" Bobbie asked. "I'm getting rid of my weed. The Police are searching the building. I think it's a drug bust." We looked outside.

The SWAT team was not concerned with the rest of the building, only Omar's apartment. Everyone came out to watch as they brought Omar out. They laid him face down on the concrete in the courtyard. "Twenty-five!" he was yelling. I walked closer until the policemen pointed the guns at me and motioned me away. "Look after Marie for me." One of the Policemen would kick his head into the concrete. Omar would raise up again, his face bloody. "Look after Marie for me, Twenty-five."

After they took Omar away, I went back to Bobbie's. "That's a whole lot of fire power for a drug bust." I said. Several ladies from the building had gathered at Bobbie's to talk about the police activity.

"That was no drug bust," someone said.

Bobbie had everyone laughing about me flushing my weed down the toilet for nothing.

"No, this was about that funeral home robbery," someone else said. "Didn't you hear about it on the news?"

"What funeral home robbery? How come I don't know anything about this?" I asked.

"Because you were in here getting high and having

sex with Bobbie. That was the night you passed out and we all saw that body of yours."

"Why rob a funeral home? They don't have a lot of money on hand, do they?"

"Embalming fluid, Twenty-five. Eight gallons of embalming fluid was taken. They make PCP from embalming fluid. You are so dumb."

Blue came down to tell me he was moving away from the Jungle. He said that things were not going well and he needed to get away while the getting was good. He warned me to do the same.

"I don't know what happened to the eight gallons of embalming fluid, Twenty-five. I really don't know, but I do know it's time to get out of the Jungle, you know what I mean?"

"Eight gallons is a lot of stuff to hide. I'm willing to bet the White boy set up Omar and Kojac, and I'm glad that I'm not involved."

"Me too, Twenty-five." He reached out to shake my hand. As we walked away in different directions, Blue turned and called out to me. "You know, Twenty-five, I sure thought you were the police." We laughed.

The receipt of the Veterans Administrations decision finally came. The findings were a disappointment. I was rated thirty percent disabled. I had anticipated the lowest possible rating. My monthly compensation was one hundred thirty-three dollars a month. They also ruled that compensation would not be paid from the time I became disabled in the Marine Corps. Instead, I would be paid from the time I stopped working for Chrysler. I did not get enough money to pay my back rent or to continue renting an apartment.

I would have to find other means of support. I knew I

had to get off drugs first. Since my attempts to clean myself up were unsuccessful, I went to the Veterans Administration Hospital's Mental Hygiene Clinic for drug rehabilitation.

The Jungle changed after Omar and Kojac left. Evelyn tried to sell drugs for awhile. Twice she called me to come over when someone came into the apartment with a gun. The second time I went to her rescue, the man had an Uzi. I managed to wrestle the gun away from the man. Then I tried to convince Evelyn that selling dope was not a good idea. Omar could handle it, I could not sell dope, and she should not sell it, because I could not provide security. Eventually, Evelyn gave up her career as the drug queen of the Jungle.

Kojac had become a legend. Several people had a fear that he would return to the Jungle to kill them. His wife Debra came to me and offered to pay me to act as her bodyguard. I assured her that Kojac had no intention of doing her any harm. She disagreed. Debra began to visit me quite often. She always had drugs and we got high together. I realized that I would have to move away from the Jungle to cure my addiction.

After Omar's drug business stopped, younger men took over the sale of Sherm in the Jungle. The alley behind Omar's apartment became known as "Sherm Alley." The alley was set up so that people could drive through to buy drugs just like a fast-food restaurant. Fistfights gave way to shootings and because of the activity in the Jungle, the police began driving through the alley with a show of force. Nearly every night there was a shooting incident. What seemed like dozens of police cars would speed through the alley with lights and sirens. This cleared the alley of buyers and pushers for awhile, but they would return after the police left.

Eventually an iron gate was placed at each end of the alley. After that, those who drove through would run into a dead end. The gate never stopped business. Drug buyers would park near the entrance to the alley then walk through to purchase the dope.

Eventually a new drug appeared on the scene. The drug users called it "rock cocaine." It seemed the drug of choice for a lot of PCP users. The sale of Sherm and angel dust decreased as more users turned to the rock. Rocks usually came in two sizes, twenty-five dollar rocks and fifty-dollar rocks. This was far more expensive than the ten-dollar Sherm or a ten-dollar bag of angel dust. The most peculiar thing about the rock was, it always made the user crave for more. The cravings were unending. Once a person began smoking it, they were willing to sell everything they had to get more.

Poor people usually could not afford to buy the twenty-five or fifty dollar rocks so they began asking the pushers to break off a "crack." The "crack" was a little piece of the twenty-five-dollar rock, and the little pieces could be sold for a dollar or more. Since most of those arrested for using rock cocaine were poor, they were arrested for the cracks instead of the rock. It was the police who began using the name "Crack" for rock cocaine.

I was first introduced to the drug when Johnnie-Reb and I attended a party. It was amazing how women loved the drug. Once they got hooked, women would do anything to obtain crack, including any sex act. Pushers took advantage.

Crack was a powerful drug. It was easy to spot a user because each user would begin selling everything they had to obtain the drug. You could see people's televisions leaving the house, furniture, jewelry and things people had worked years to obtain, all sold to the drug pushers or to obtain money to buy the drug.

Crack would change whole neighborhoods. My heart sank as I saw single mothers being evicted along with their children. People who were otherwise honest would suddenly become creatures who would steal from or sell their own parents for crack. Some women would offer their children for the drug. If someone was intentionally trying to destroy a generation, they had succeeded.

The pushers became younger, the users grew older. Older women, who had earned the respect of children, would now offer their bodies to those same children for crack. Children, watching the adults throw their lives away on crack, eventually lost all respect for their elders. The crack dealers ruled the streets. Children turned to gangs to find what they could no longer get at home. Otherwise nice neighborhoods would completely change to gang territory in a matter of days.

I had begun using crack after being introduced to it at the party. Because I could maintain self-control in using the drug, several women enjoyed getting high with me. The women told me that I was different when using the drug because most men became uncontrollably paranoid, they could not fight the urge to get more after the dope was gone, and I never came up with any weird sexual request.

I did have a certain level of control, but I also experienced the urges. I did not like crack because, to me, it was the closest thing to demonic possession I had ever seen. No crack user controlled crack. Like an evil spirit, crack had a mind of its own. Once you got hooked, the drug was in control. No matter how much you loved a person or no matter how much they loved you, once they were on crack, they could no longer be trusted.

Part of the goal of martial arts training is "being master of your own impulses." After I began feeling the loss of control, I stopped using the drug. Later, I checked myself into the Brentwood Veterans Administrations mental hospital to get myself completely off drugs.

Although I was hospitalized, the Veterans Administration still refused to raise my disability payments. I had no income to afford a place to live if I left the hospital. While I was still in the hospital, I managed to get a job at the Veterans Administration Regional office in Los Angeles. My job as a file clerk did not pay enough to afford an apartment.

Larry Davis and Jack Vance were other veterans who worked as clerks. Since our positions were so low, it was astounding how the other workers looked down on us. We were almost forced to stick together because the other black men who had better-paying positions would not speak to us at all. It was a weird place to work.

Larry had a room in a cheap hotel across from MacArthur Park, near downtown Los Angeles. After I was released from the hospital, Larry helped me to get a room in the hotel. Our paychecks were barely enough to cover the rent. I was lucky in that I had the hundred and thirty-three dollars compensation to help me survive. The place was roach-and rat-infested but it was all we could afford. I always ended up lending Larry and Jack some of my compensation checks so that we could eat. After work I would go up on the roof to practice martial arts. Larry was interested in learning, and I began to teach him.

Jack lived in a cheap hotel in another part of Los Angeles. When they went up on his rent, he moved to the same place as me and Larry. The three of us practiced every night. As part of our training, we began running around the lake in MacArthur Park. As time passed, my stamina grew.

At first we ran around the lake once a day, then twice. I kept increasing the number of times I made it around until Larry and Jack would stop and sit on the benches waiting for me to finish. After a while, they began to go to the hotel, shower, and then come back to see me complete my run. Eventually they told me it was useless trying to run with me. I got to where I could run around the lake twenty-seven times. Since Jack had a steady girlfriend and Larry had several, I felt that I owned my stamina to me not having sex. Larry was popular everywhere. He introduced me to several ladies who lived at the hotel. None of them suited my taste.

My moving into the place created problems for Larry from the beginning. We were all due at work at eight o'clock each morning. I was glad to have the job, and I was determined to be on time. Larry, Jack, and I caught the bus on Wilshire Boulevard near the hotel. The Supervisor knew we lived at the same place yet I was always on time.

After Jack moved in, we caught the bus together, and the both of us were always on time. Larry had been arriving late since he first got the job. His excuse had been the bus did not run that early. The supervisor did not like the fact that he had been played. He began to show a dislike for Larry and treated him with disrespect.

As Larry became better at martial arts, his confidence grew; he wanted to use his skills on the supervisor. I advised him against it. Larry was disappointed with his life. He seemed to become more disappointed after I was introduced to his cousin Sheryl. Sheryl as a very special lady. She looked like a beauty queen, she owned a business that provided bus transportation for trips to Las Vegas, she bought new cars every year, and when she was younger, she had won several beauty contests. One contest had earned her the title, "Miss Compton."

Sheryl would drop by from time to time to check on her cousin. After Larry introduced us, he told me about her accomplishments and about the type of men she liked. I told him how special I thought she was and I wanted to go out with her. Larry assured me that Sheryl would never agree to go out with men in our condition. We had the lowest-paying jobs and we lived in that rat-infested place. Her dates were always rich guys who drove expensive cars. Larry was amazed when Sheryl invited me to dinner at her stylish apartment. He was shocked to find that I spent the night. Soon I was driving Sheryl's new car. I also accompanied her on trips to Las Vegas.

Since she already had a fabulous apartment, Larry became furious when a relative gave Sheryl a house. After that, his whole conversation was about how his family treated him differently. "Here I am staying in this roach- and rat-infested hotel, and they give her a fucking house. It's not fair. No one ever did anything for me," he complained. Larry's anger grew daily. When the supervisor confronted him again about being late, Larry cursed him out and walked off the job. He decided he could live off his martial arts kills.

While Jack and I kept our jobs, Larry's new profession became snatching purses. We could not talk him into coming back to work. After all, he now had more money than Jack and me, and he did not work. He met a girl named Linda after she had seen him make a daring robbery, and escape an exciting police pursuit. Linda was a pretty girl who had the facial scars to show that she had led a rough life. She had done time in jail. After they met, she moved in with Larry, and they worked together stealing and robbing.

Later, Larry met a White prostitute called Popcorn. She needed a pimp, and Larry decided to take the job.

Sheryl informed us about a job opening with the Southern California Rapid Transit District. I applied for the job. Jack did not feel confident to try driving the big buses and Larry was very happy being a pimp.

Linda's information came at the right time President Carter was out of office, and President Reagan was making a lot of changes. Before, Federal Employees never had to worry about being laid off. Because of President Reagan's changes, new employees found themselves being laid off. I was one of them. There was a lot of gossip about how they would find a way to keep the Whites, and they did.

Driving the bus was the job of my dreams. Women liked the uniform, and I came home each day with a pocket filled with phone numbers. As long as there were no problems on the job, I never had to worry about supervision. I got a chance to see how beautiful California was and I made good money. Before long, I had moved out of the hotel. I found a place in West Los Angeles with a swimming pool, tennis court, and gym. I was living better now than I had in Detroit.

I visited Larry in the hospital after Sheryl informed me that he had been stabbed. Larry told me that, his girlfriend Linda had stabbed him after she became jealous over some of his other whores. The doctor said he was lucky to be alive because the knife wound was less than a quarter-inch from his heart.

I visited the hotel to talk to Linda who gave me the more believable story. She said, that, Larry had become obsessed with using the martial arts that I had taught him he had kicked her in the face and broken her jaw on two separate occasions. She had warned him that if he ever kicked her again, she would get him while he slept. After his last attack, she waited until he was asleep, then stabbed him in the chest. She said Larry woke up and chased her for nearly ten blocks with the knife still in his chest.

Linda, Popcorn, and Larry were still together the last time I visited him at the hotel. He also had four other girls and two big transvestites in the room. I felt that it was time for me to stay away. The next thing I heard about Larry was that he had used martial arts to kill a man in MacArthur Park and was sent to prison.

When I went to the Jungle to visit Evelyn, the Jungle had changed and Evelyn had changed. The Jungle was now filled with people from Belize. I found it strange meeting Black people with accents I was not familiar with. Several families from that country had moved into Omar's old apartment building. Evelyn had become a close friend of a lady named Frances. Frances was a devout Christian. She had converted Evelyn. Both of them went to church every Sunday and Bible study on Wednesdays. All thoughts of dealing drugs or being a drug queen had vanished. Evelyn's conversations now revolved around the Bible. Frances would accompany Evelyn on her visits to see Omar. They would hold prayer sessions for him. Occasionally I got to talk to him on the phone. I apologized for not coming to see him. I explained to him that I could not force myself to go near a prison. My brief experience being incarcerated still gave me nightmares.

"I understand, little brother." Omar would say.

Frances was married to an Army veteran. She had an eighteen-year-old daughter, Shawn, who was pregnant. Shawn was half-White. Frances had previously been married to a White Army Officer. She said she had divorced him because he became impotent. She had also experienced a lot of racial problems during the marriage. On one occasion, she had overheard a White officer's wife complain about the seating arrangements at a dinner they had been invited to. "I know you're not going to seat me next to the nigger," the White woman had said. The man's impotence and accumulation of racial incidents had caused the marriage to break up.

Things were not going well with her second marriage, either. Life with a Black man was far too different than the life she had been accustomed to. He found it hard to keep a job after his discharge from the Army and it was obvious she was out of place in the Jungle.

Frances was special. I had the actual experience of losing my breath when I first saw her. Her face glowed and her body was indescribable. Our mutual attraction was hard to ignore. I tried hard not to stare at her, and she would steal glances at me whenever we were together at Evelyn's.

Evelyn asked me why I did not meet her husband, get together with him, and go out on the town. I explained that I did not want to know her husband or to associate with him in any way. I liked his wife too much. I told Evelyn how special I thought Frances was and, given the chance, she would be mine.

Shawn came to visit Evelyn every time I came over. Evelyn told me that she was attracted to me. I told her I could never bring myself to go with an eighteen-year-old, legal age or no. Being as strong in the Christian faith as she was, Evelyn was shocked when Frances admitted she was attracted to me. The only communication she had with her husband was arguments. She went to church; he drank.

I told Evelyn the reason the man constantly argued with her was because he knew she was way out of his class and there was nothing he could do about it. The arguments got worse. Frances would sometimes come over crying about something stupid her husband had said and, before long, he left home and did not return. After the separation, Frances and I began to talk. Like her husband, I knew that she was way out of my league as well.

Just walking down the street in a pair of shorts caused men to stumble over things looking back at her. Others fell off bikes and drivers had accidents. Whenever they went out together, Evelyn would return with stories about their adventures.

"You, my boy," Evelyn would say, "should bottle whatever you have, I keep telling you. Along with all the women in the Jungle, you got a mother and daughter liking you."

Frances told me that, she would never again date a man who did not go to church. I began accompanying her to church. I knew that going to church would not be enough, though. She needed someone she could look up to and respect, someone who had made something out of his life and, had stability. She inspired me to start improving myself.

I enrolled in West Los Angeles College. I studied Computer Science and was happy beyond belief when I made an A in the class. I also began working as an extra in the movies. I auditioned for the movie *The Last Dragon*. However, I was so excited, and I got stage fright during my audition. I continued my schooling and did extra work to gain movie experience. With her inspiration, I was pleased with the progress I was making with my life.

Six
The Black Knight

I purchased a big beautiful motorcycle and a black helmet that had the other bus drivers calling me "Darth Vader." Frances took a job at some factory near downtown Los Angeles. After a while, she moved out of the Jungle into an area called West Covina.

On one of my visits, Frances was very sad to tell me that the White man who owned the factory had asked her to marry him. She had accepted because he was very rich. She said that she felt sad because of the problems Black men have trying to make a living in a place where the cards were stacked against them. I told her that I understood. I could not blame anyone for wanting financial security, and I had learned that there was too much control over the lives of Black men.

One lesson I learned in life was that poverty should be avoided at all costs and, as a Black man in America, I knew I could end up living in the park at any time. I was happy to have spent some time with someone as special as her and I had learned not to cling to anyone or anything.

Doing extra work in the movies was exciting. I enjoyed speeding around on my motorcycle from one set to the next. I met James Earl Jones and Rae Dawn Chong on the set of a movie called *City Limits.* I actually bumped into Debby Boone on the set of a movie called *Sins of the*

Past. When Richard Pryor was making *Brewster's Millions* I was a team captain. I could sign up other extras.

By this time I was in church a lot less and at the strip clubs a lot more. I had gained the same popularity with dancers that I had in Detroit. The thing about strip clubs was, every time you think you've met the world's most beautiful woman, you end up meeting someone more beautiful. In addition, there was always excitement in the clubs. I remember one night a dancer took my motorcycle helmet and did such an act with it, I wanted to frame the thing so that I could always remember that dance.

Another night, I sat right in front of the stage hypnotized by the performances. The women seemed to be dancing for me, because they had my full attention. One man became so angry that he jumped up yelling, "What the fuck is going on here. Are all of these bitches dancing just for him? Why don't they dance for everybody?" The girls, the customers, and I were cracking up as the bouncers escorted him from the bar. I never felt more proud.

On another night, I was wearing a short leather jacket when a big guy seated at the table next to mine said, "Give me that coat." I looked around at him and smiled, thinking he was joking.

"I said, give me that coat," the man repeated.

I looked at the man again and saw that he was serious. I turned my attention to the dancer.

"You think you're going to get out of here with that coat, but you're not."

At that point I removed my jacket and laid it across my legs. When I did, the man made a leap and tried to grab it. My anger overwhelmed me and I began to beat him unmercifully. Before the bouncers pulled me off, we were on the stage with me banging his head against the floor over and over.

None of the girls made me forget about Frances, until I met Vanessa Nathan. When I first saw her, not only did I lose my breath, my mind went blank for a few seconds. There was no match for her face, her body, or the way she danced. Vanessa had the physical control of a yoga master. It was easy to talk to her because she was from Detroit. She drove a Cadillac Seville.

Vanessa wasn't looking to be a movie star, but she was excited about getting a chance to be an extra in Richard Pryor's movie. As a team captain, she was impressed by me being able to get her in. We spent a lot of time talking about being in the movie together. I was to pick her up on the morning we were due on the set. I had not planned to go to the bar before then, but I wanted to watch her dance.

When I entered the club, one of the dancers approached me and asked if I had heard about Vanessa. "Heard what?" I asked.

"She's dead."

I laughed, "Vanessa's not dead. I just saw Vanessa last night." "It happened late last night," the dancer said. "She was in this place that got robbed. The robbers did not want to leave any witnesses, so, everyone was blown away with a shotgun, including Vanessa."

After, I found the story to be true, and learned Vanessa's death had something to do with crack. I remained sick for days. I missed out on the filming of *Brewster's Millions* and eventually quit working for the bus company. All I wanted to do was to go back home to Alabama.

The only thing that kept me from leaving Los Angeles right away was that the death rate surrounding crack was phenomenal. One did not need to be a user to end up getting killed; all you had to do was to be around it.

Again, I thought about my wife Mary. Again, I felt guilty about bringing her to such a place. I knew that Mary loved to get high and she loved cocaine. If everyone was using crack, more than likely Mary was, too. Before I left, I had to find her, and if she was on the drug, I had to get her away from it.

I had Mary's address on 91st Street, and I had been through the neighborhood before. It was a nice clean neighborhood with neat apartments. That was a year before. Things had changed. After dark, most of the people who drove down the street were looking for crack.

The street was becoming overcrowded with pushers. As one man drove slowly by waiting for a pusher to approached, he found himself being rushed by young men on both sides of his car. Both of the men were trying to sell their crack. The two young men began to argue about who would get to make the sale. The buyer got nervous and drove farther up the block; the young men continued arguing.

"Hey man, you guys work for Roy. That's our end of the block down there. You don't have no business rushing our customers."

"What do you mean our end. Nigger, that was my customer. Y'all can't tell nobody where to sell dope. Hell, the street belongs to everybody."

"Oh yeah? You just wait. We'll see about that." The young man walked off, motioning to his coworkers to follow. The men went to the apartment of a woman in her early thirties. She didn't have the appearance of a drug dealer. However, she was one of the biggest dealers in the neighborhood.

"Yeah, Lila," the young man says after they are inside. "The same shit is happening. We have to tell them every night to stay on their end of the block. Every night, they do the same thing—they keep stealing our customers."

Lila got up and walked over to a closet. "Don't worry, if talk won't help, got something that will." She began pulling weapons out of the closet and passing them to the men.

"Take these. Go back out there and back them up. Make sure they understand if any one of them crosses the center of this block again, that's their ass."

The young men took the weapons and went back out on the street. They formed a line and walked up the block like a police riot squad. One of the men fired into the air. The other pushers began to run.

"That's right, run, muther-fuckers and remember, from now on you bastards stay on that end. Anybody who crosses the middle of this block selling dope is a dead man."

Roy is the dealer on the front end of the block. His workers run to his apartment to tell him about the incident. Roy began pacing the floor. "OK, that's the way they want to play it, huh? Well, you guys don't worry, well just close down for the night. Tomorrow, it'll be a different story. I promise you, you'll never have to run again."

After that, most of the pushers were armed. There were frequent shootouts and a lot of young men died. The street was smoky, as if there had been a gun fight as I slowly drove my motorcycle looking for Mary's apartment. The way the place had changed amazed me. I kept motioning the men away who rushed up to my bike to sell crack. I could not find Mary's place. I decided to call her the next day to get the correct address.

Mary's apartment was between Lila's and Roy's. When I returned the next night, I heard a lot of fumbling around when I knocked on the door. "Who is it?" someone yelled.

"It's Twenty-five," I answered.

"Go to the back door."

I walked around the building to the back door and knocked again.

"Who is it?"

"Twenty-five."

A really nervous big guy jerked opened the door holding a pistol. "What do you want?"

"Is this Mary's apartment?"

"Speak up, nigger," the man yelled, pointing the gun close to my face. "What do you want?"

I quickly twisted the gun from his hand and kicked him over the kitchen table. Another man ran into the kitchen from the front of the house, pulling a pistol from his belt. I was already aiming at his head before he could get it out.

"I wouldn't try it," I said, shaking my head and smiling.

The man dropped his gun, raised his hands, and backed up against the wall. Another man rushed into the room. He saw me and stopped. "Brother-in law!" he yelled. "Calm down you fools. It's my brother-law, Twenty-five."

The man was Mary's brother, J. T. He yelled to Mary, "Hey Sis, You'll never guess who's here, it's Twenty-five."

Mary was in her bedroom getting high with J. T. and a man named Easy. When J. T. introduced me as Mary's husband, the man excused himself and said he was going home. When I asked what was happening, I learned that Mary was indeed a heavy crack user. She still worked for Transamerica and supported the habit by allowing Easy and his brother to deal crack from her apartment. Easy's brother was preparing the stuff on the stove in the kitchen. J. T. was pushing dope on the street. He sometimes worked for Lila.

In Detroit, J. T. had been a well-known martial artist and a player. It was hard for me to understand how he had ended up in Los Angeles with a crack habit and working for young punks to support his habit. Easy had said he had to leave to go home but I sensed he and Mary lived together and that he had made the statement for my benefit. I was right.

I began visiting often. My plan was to protect Mary, gain her confidence by smoking crack with her, and then suggest that we quit together. On my visits, I got to know Easy. He was another ex-con who bragged about time he spent in San Quentin. He tried to act tough, but it was easy to tell he was nowhere near as tough as Omar, Kojac, or any of the gang members in the Jungle.

Like Frances's husband, he realized Mary was way out of his class. He had heard about me and had been impressed by the stories Mary and J. T. had told. Nearly all of his conversations were about prison life. Easy, Mary, J. T. and I sat for hours talking and smoking crack. Easy made money selling dope, then smoked everything he made. The pushers liked Mary and respected her as much as a crack addict could be respected. As they got to know me, they would ask me behind Easy's back, "Why don't you take her out of here, man? She don't belong here."

I didn't get to talk to Mary alone much, but when I did, I would throw out hints about giving up crack. She seemed to be in agreement. However, I knew there was no way to quit in the atmosphere she was in. As she said she was waiting for a knight in shining armor to come and save her.

I arrived one night to find J. T. beaten so badly he

was unrecognizable. He had been selling dope for Lila and had smoked up the money he was supposed to turn in. Another time, he had smoked the crack he was supposed to be selling and had substituted a piece of soap for crack and sold it to a buyer. The man had returned with a shotgun, broke down the door, and came into the apartment looking for him. It was a sad experience seeing a fellow marital artist end up this way.

With my frequent visits, Easy began asking me if I wanted to join him in dealing crack. He said with the money that we were spending, we could easily become rich selling instead of smoking. I told him my religion would not allow me to sell dope to another human being. I could deal with hurting myself, but harming another person was bad karma.

Easy had a sister who came by to purchase dope. He did not like the fact that his sister liked me after he had been introduced. She came by looking for me, and I had an excuse to spend more time at Mary's.

This situation made a drastic change when Easy and I were sitting in the kitchen talking. Several of the young pushers gathered on the back porch, unaware that Easy and I were in the kitchen. "Easy ain't shit, man" one of the men said.

"I know it man, I wish Twenty-five would take Mary and get her the fuck out of here. That nigger Easy don't even have a place to say. He keeps his sorry ass in Mary's apartment bragging about San Quentin. I'll bet he was somebody's bitch in San Quentin."

"Let's go outside, man," I said.

"No, Twenty-five, let them niggers talk, I don't give a fuck. I'll remember."

From then on, Easy was uneasy every time I came over. He did try harder to hold on to some money for the dope he sold. He drove by to pick me up one day in a Cadillac, as if he were trying to impress me. When I inquired about the car, he said a woman had offered to let him keep the car for two days in exchange for fifty dollars worth of crack. He was about to return the car and collect the money. I would follow on my bike to give him a ride home.

When we got to the woman's apartment, her husband was there angry about what she had done. When the woman paid Easy the money, the man walked out of the door telling Easy he was going to blow his head off as soon as he walked outside. The fear on Easy's face made me laugh. He was really afraid to leave the woman's apartment.

"Let's go," I said.

"I ain't going out there, that fool is outside with a shotgun."

"What are you going to do? Stay here for good?"

"You can leave if you want to, Twenty-five. I ain't no fool."

I grabbed my helmet and walked out of the door. The man was standing there with shotgun. I looked at him and smiled as I walked to my bike. I could tell the man did not want to kill anyone. He was angry and hurt over what his wife had done, but he wasn't ready to go to prison. I got on the bike and rode up to the door blowing the horn. The man got into a truck and left. "Come on, Easy," I called. "It's safe." Easy peeked around the door, sweating profusely and trembling.

The next time I visited, Easy was in the hospital; he had just been shot. The story was, Easy had gone out to a car to sell a rock when a man shot him, took his money, and his dope. Some of the workers recognized the man as a rival gang member. While Easy was in the hospital, the gang drove to the shooter's neighborhood and located his house. They got out of their cars and began firing into the house. Before they finished, they nearly brought the entire house to the ground.

While Easy was in the hospital, I had two days to talk to Mary. I never mentioned getting back together; I did preach about giving up crack and starting a new life. On the second day, Easy came home. He was furious because Mary had not picked him up at the hospital. He was afraid to confront me. He calmly talked about how he had been shot. I listened for a while, then went home.

The phone was ringing when I got home. Lila was on the other end. "Listen, Twenty-five," she said. "I have a message from Mary. That Nigger Easy is tripping out. She said after you left, he played Russian Roulette with her. She's about to leave, and she wants to know if it's OK for her to stay with you."

"Sure," I said. "But she doesn't know where I live."

"Don't worry, she'll find you."

Mary knew that I lived in West Los Angeles, but she had no address. I was worried that she would not be able to find the place. I went out walking, knowing West Los Angeles was a big place. There was very little chance of her finding my apartment with just luck.

My assumption was wrong. After I had walked for blocks and blocks, I looked up to see her walking toward me.

I called Jack Vance to tell him that I may be having problems with Easy and his gang. Jack came over to watch my back. I expected gunplay from Easy and the gang, but when Jack spotted Easy driving by my apartment, he was alone. For two nights, Easy drove by and kept going. On the third night, Jack drove next to him, looked him in the eyes, and laughed. Easy sped off.

After that, I began driving down 91st Street on my

bike. Easy was walking toward the street when I made my second trip through the neighborhood. He spotted me and ran into the apartment to get his bother. I parked my bike, took off my helmet, and got off to meet the two of them as they came toward me. Easy stayed behind his big brother. Each one carried a pistol. They walked toward me really fast, at first, expecting their gang members to follow. They slowed down after looking around and seeing the men were staying back.

There was the loud sound of tires burning rubber as Jack's car jumped the curb and stopped beside Easy and his brother. Jack pointed his Uzi at them. "Twenty-five don't believe in guns. I do. You can drop them and play with him, or keep them and play with me. How do you want it?" Both guns fell to the ground. Easy began backing up, his brother came forward and attempted to throw a punch. I blocked the punch and began to deliver punishing kicks and punches until he fell to the ground unconscious. Easy turned and ran. I never saw him again. However, it was not long before I heard that he had been killed in a gang-related shooting.

Kicking the crack habit wasn't going to be easy for Mary. I truly had no problem quitting because, having kept myself in shape for martial arts most of my life, I felt guilty every time I smoked. I hated the thought that crack had a mind of its own and it was in charge. I also loved sharp cars and clothes. If I was going to waste my money, a sharp apartment, a sharp car, and sharp clothes would have been my primary choices.

I planned for us to gradually quit. I told Mary that my plan was to move back to Alabama; however, I would never go near my mother with a drug habit. My philosophy was, exercise could cure anything if you work out so hard that you have no energy left. All you will want to do is sleep. Mary and I began running up the big hill on La Brea Avenue every day, practicing martial arts, and going for long walks.

Mary was real skinny when she moved in with me, but after a few runs up that hill, she had nice shapely legs in no time. We both agreed that being away from the drug scene made it easier to quit. Unfortunately the craving for crack stays with you for years after you quit. If you have a weak mind, you're hooked for life. I was glad that I had experienced the drug for myself. That way, no one could ever talk me or trick me into using it.

My plan for gradual withdrawal came to an abrupt end when Mary had a seizure one night. Her heart stopped beating and her breathing stopped. I don't know how long I spent giving her artificial respiration, pounding her chest, and praying to God that, if he let her live, I would never use crack again or let her use it again.

When Mary came to, she did not realize what had happened. She viciously attacked me when I began to flush the crack that remained down the toilet. It took a long time to convince her that she had actually died. I finally convinced her after I told her that I would never use crack again, and if she did, we would have to separate.

We both quit without any problems. Sometimes it was hard to sleep without dreaming about the drug. To me crack was the closet thing to being possessed by a demon that I had ever encountered.

Mary and I had never agreed to get back together or to stay together, but months passed. We both worked out very hard every day. After I got into excellent physical condition, I began to feel like my old self. I looked for a martial arts school and began to train under grand master Hee Ill Cho. Mary began taking hapkido. She got a job at a bank in Beverly Hills, and our lives normalized.

Grand master Cho eventually gave me my own class. After a while, I talked Mary into going to grand master Cho's school. I told grand master Cho about my plan to move to Alabama and to open my own school. He gave me advice on what I should do. It was 1998 when we finally moved to Alabama. It was after grand master Cho left Los Angeles and moved the world headquarters of the Action International Martial Arts Association to Albuquerque, New Mexico.

During the years I was away from home, I ran up big telephone bills calling my mother weekly and having long conversations with her. She loved old "Tarzan" movies. I taped a lot of them preparing to watch them with her when I got home.

Before I made it home, my mother began to tell me that she was worried because she felt that she was losing her memory. Later we learned she had Alzheimer's Disease. Mary and I dropped everything to move to Alabama.

My mother remembered me when I got home, even though she did not know my sisters and brothers who were already there. I was terribly upset about her illness and sad that we never got a chance to watch the movies I had on tape. Soon she did not know anyone, and her condition deteriorated to the point she had to be placed in a nursing home.

It his hard to describe Alabama without using the world "evil." It is never a surprise to hear people from all over the world speak of how evil it is. From the time I left home in the Sixties, until I moved back, the mention of my being from Alabama got the same response, "Yeah, I went through Alabama once. Believe me, I got through there as fast as I could." Nothing anybody could say about the place could describe actually living there.

Mary and I had arranged to rent a house from Los

Angeles. When we got to the house, some White men were shampooing the carpet. We told them that we would leave and return after they finished. However, we could hear one of the men remark, "That's good enough for them." The men left without completing their work.

There were only a few Black people in the neighborhood. Some of the White people were friendly others would turn their heads to avoid looking or speaking. In some businesses, Whites went out of their way to show their dislike for Blacks. Just like in the Sixties, some Whites would wait on other Whites first or pretend to be busy doing other things to make you wait. In one copy shop, one lady would take pennies out of the register to count them while I waited.

On weekends we would visit my sister in Birmingham. Her husband rented a booth at a flea market. On one of our visits, a White family noticed my brother-in-law sold children's bikes cheaper than the rest of the vendors at the same location.

"Hey, these same bikes cost five dollars more at the other shops," a young lady replied. "Maybe we should buy them here."

"Yeah, but you'd be buying Black," was the reply.

In a conversation with a repairman who came to the house, we learned that interracial marriages were illegal in the State of Alabama. The man was upset and anxious to see the law changed because he was married to a White woman. Mary was amazed; I felt like I had gone back in time.

I contacted the Board of Education in an effort to teach tae kwon do classes with the school system. The people I spoke to did not know or pretended not to know what tae kwon do was. I tried to teach classes with the Continuing Education Program at Alabama State University, and found myself getting the runaround from the man in charge of the program.

I began teaching tae kwon do classes at Houston Hill Community Center, Grace Christian Academy, and then Floyd's Community Center. I never got enough students to help my mother out financially. Eventually I tried working as a security guard. As soon as I began working, an old nightmare came back to haunt me. The State of Michigan issued wage withholding papers for my salary. Although it had been nearly thirty years, the same case that originally caused me to lose my job was reopened.

They were still trying to collect child support for Antoine. The irony is, Antoine was now under court order to pay child support himself. I began writing to President Clinton this time in a desperate effort to have this case investigated. The courts began the same threats that had ruined our lives in 1976.

Besides President Clinton, I wrote to the Department of Justice, the FBI, the Department of Health and Human Services, the Family Independence Agency, the Alabama State Bar, the Michigan State Bar, and the NAACP. Eventually I found out that lawyers avoided child support cases. I saved a letter from Johnnie Cochran's office turning down the case and advising me to seek another attorney. I realized that there was no way I could convince anyone that the court had acted improperly.

I began focusing on the fact that Minnie was married to someone else. I questioned how a married woman could collect child support from someone else's husband. I needed proof that Minnie was married and proof that I had been refused a blood test and incarcerated. Mary and I had been nearly driven insane. The more we tried to seek help, the more threats the court sent.

After I continued to write President Clinton, he asked Congressman Terry Everette to investigate the case. After Congressman Everette began looking into the case, the court found, that while working for Chrysler, all of my salary had been taken because they had been collecting on two cases. I had voluntarily had support payments taken from my paycheck for my children. The additional payments the court ordered for Minnie consumed my entire check. Since this was illegal, the court protected itself by dismissing the case where I was voluntarily supporting my children.

The court could not come up with a reason for incarcerating me without allowing me to have a blood test, so they changed Minnie's child support case to an alimony case. They then began sending letters stating that I owed over twenty-five thousand dollars in alimony. Again, I began writing the President asking how I could owe another man's wife alimony without knowing it.

Eventually I took a chance and paid someone to look through the records to find a marriage license for Minnie and a man named Rudy. God was with me again. I was sent a Wayne County Marriage License for Minnie L. Brown and Rudolph Eady. The two of them had been married on Sept. 28th 1970. State file number 70971.

I also managed to get a letter from the third Judicial Circuit of Michigan, dated January 9, 2001, stating my Judgment for Divorce from Minnie, "had specific language which shows no alimony was to be paid by either party."

The court was not willing to admit any wrongdoing. After I provided Congressman Terry Everett with a copy of Minnie and Rudy's marriage license and the letter showing I was never ordered to pay alimony, the court changed the case once again, this time from an alimony case back to a child support case.

I was summoned to court again for the child support case, knowing the only reason was to give the false impression that the court had acted properly. Unlike the time I was incarcerated, I went to court this time with a copy of Minnie's marriage license and another request for a blood test. "We're not going to give you a blood test for a thirty-year-old case," the Friend of the Court representative said. I told him that I had a right to have blood test.

The man talked Minnie into dropping the case. He advised me to leave it alone if I did not want to end up in jail. I notified the Michigan State Bar, the Alabama State Bar, and Congressman Terry Everett. I produced a letter sent by Congressman Everett dated January 30, 2001, that read:

> Dear Mr. Brown:
>
> Thank you for letting me know about your efforts to clear up an alleged debt which the child support enforcement authorities are collecting. You sent a copy of a letter from the Michigan Family Independence Agency, dated July 21, 2002, that clearly said you do not owe child support, and that child support case (number 19666-044693DM) was paid in full and is closed.
>
> You also sent a copy of a letter from the Third Judicial Circuit of Michigan, dated January 9, 2001, which states that your Judgment of Divorce "has specific language which shows no alimony was to be paid by either party." Nonetheless, the court thought you had a child support debt due, and they said they are scheduling a hearing.
>
> I appreciate this opportunity to be of assistance to you in this matter. I have shared your letter with officials at the US Department of Health and Human Services,

and have asked them to give you every cooperation and consideration in settling this. I have also asked if they can suggest a lawyer who will represent you in the hearing.

I will write to let you know as soon as I receive any response to my inquiries on your behalf. In the meantime, if you have any further questions or information you need to give me, please talk with Mrs. Victoria Ebell in my Washington office. For details on legislation and other useful information, I invite you to visit my website at http://www.house.gov/everett/. With best whishes."

The letter was signed, "Terry Everett."

My request for the court to investigate misconduct was ignored. After I represented the proof, the Alabama State bar recognized court misconduct but did not offer representation, stating I needed a Michigan lawyer for the case.

The Michigan State Bar referred me to a Ledland Prince at 3000 Town Center, Suite 698, Southfield, Michigan,48075. I called Mr. Prince's office and provided him with the information in the case. I was under the impression that Mr. Prince was working on my case until I received a letter from his office dated May 8, 2002. The letter said, "Dear Mr. Brown: Please remove my name from our fax distribution list." I never got the money back that had been taken by the court or any restitution for my illegal incarceration, the loss of my job, or the inhuman harassment that covered a thirty-year period.

I was sure that divine intervention could help to resolve the problems I had with the court. I began going to church. Mary would go sometimes, but she held on to her belief that most of the people who went to church were hypocrites. We both joined the Dexter Avenue King Memorial Baptist Church. Reverend Michael Fox Thurman was the Pastor, and we became good friends.

I began attending bible study classes and gained a new respect for the Christian religion in discussions with others who attended the classes. Dr. Martin Luther King had once been the pastor of the church, and I had always held an interest in the place after an experience I had there during the civil rights movement. Reverend Thurman eventually began studying tae kwon do with me.

Mary and I were happy to finally be free of the harassment and for the chance to start over. I continued teaching tae kwon do classes at the community centers, and participated in summer programs with the children. The house we had rented went up for sale, we were given an opportunity to purchase it, and I was excited about owning a home.

Overdue student loans prevented us from being able to use my Veteran's Certificate of Eligibility to purchase a home. We also became victims of predatory lending when, after we had been approved for the loan, the lenders raised the interest rate twice before we closed the deal. The normal rate during that time was around three percent. We were told that, because of past-due student loans, our rate would be sixteen percent for one year, and then we could refinance at the normal rate. Mary was angry and did not want to close the deal. I convinced her that Black people did not get fair treatment in the South and that we were lucky to get the house at any rate. I told her that the year would pass quickly, and soon we could own the home with a normal interest rate.

The predatory lender was Associated. After the year was up Mary was looking forward to getting the rate reduced. Associates informed us that the company had been sold to Citifinancial Mortgage and this company would not honor Associates' promises to reduce the interest rate. Before we could see other means to refinance the house, the Department of Education took my twenty-five hundred dollar student loan, added eight thousand dollars interest, then began taking my disability check. We found ourselves with more bills than we could handle. When I made an attempt to stop the deductions from my disability checks because I was disabled, the reply was, I was not disabled by the Department of Education's standards.

Seven
The New Name for Niggers

In November 2003, Mary and I were hired by the United States Postal Service as "casual employees." The Postal Service hired temporary workers for the Christmas holidays. My tae kwon do classes at the community centers did not pay enough for us to cover our bills and "casual employment" sounded like what I was looking for. I could work part time and continue teaching my classes.

Everyone was nice when we went to orientation. We were assigned our jobs and shifts, and told we would be treated with dignity and respect. Mary and I did not get the same shift because my employment was held up when I presented my discharge papers from the U.S. Marine Corps showing I was a Disabled Veteran. I presented my Medical Board Report from the Marine Corps, and convinced the people from Human Resources that my disabilities would not prevent me from doing "casual" work. After my employment was approved, there were no more positions on the shift that Mary had been assigned.

The supervisor for my shift came in to give a speech during orientation. He was a big Black man with a loud voice. His attitude came across as arrogant and disrespectful. He talked about what he would and would not tolerate on his shift. He seemed to be trying to scare us and no one in the group wanted to work under his supervision. Those who had worked for the postal service before told the rest of us that this was a supervisor no one wanted to work for. He was always rude, he always used foul language, and it was hard to find a more unpleasant person.

I did not feel that I would have any problems, because I was willing to follow the rules and to do a good job. Others warned me that they would rather give up the job rather than to work for him. The human resources representatives made excuses for his behavior. "He may be a little rough," they would say. "But he loves his job and the job is very important to him." A woman named Judy and I were assigned to his shift.

I found the term "casual employment" to be terribly misleading after I got on the job. I was thinking I would have time to keep up my tae kwon do classes while working part time for the United States Postal Service. After being hired, I came to find out the casual employees on this job were required to work six days per week up to twelve hours a day. Casual employees did not get any holidays off and had no employee rights or benefits. The supervisors had adopted a program of pushing the casual employees as hard as possible to get as much work out of them as they could. Since the casual employees worked for less than half the pay the career employees made, the supervisors bragged about big bonuses they received for pushing them. I soon learned that in reality, "casual employment" was an experiment in slave labor conducted by this particular branch of the United States Postal Service.

Work at the main post office in Montgomery, Alabama, was like taking a trip into the past. In reality, one could see what it was like during slavery. My supervisor played the role of a slave who had been promoted to overseer. His actions gave the impression that, the more abusive he was to Blacks, the more acceptable he was to Whites. I personally felt that he was a reincarnated slave. He was especially abusive to Blacks, and the abuse was extreme when any White person was present. Most of the time, all of the "casual employees" were Black. The only reasons they accepted the job and the treatment were they could not find other work, they did not know what they were getting into, or they felt that if they accepted the abuse long enough, they could one day get career employment.

His white counterpart was not as abusive, but the two of them seemed to be competing to see who could be more disrespectful. The two of them constantly yelled at, cursed and threatened to fire the "casuals," as they called them. Although the White man did not really like the Black one, the two of them sometimes got together and bragged about their abusive treatment of the casuals.

My supervisor had a White girlfriend who also worked for the Postal Service. His attitude changed when he was with her. He seemed to enjoy showing her off, disrespecting Black women and proclaiming that he would not have a Black woman. When she was not around, all of his sexual advances were to Black women.

I made friends with a lady named Jen. She had arthritis and was visibly in pain after working a few hours. We began talking when she noticed me limping badly like her. We both began the workdays okay, but before the twelve hours were up, we were both limping badly. I became upset after I noticed that my supervisor seemed to actually enjoy the woman's pain. The more she limped about, the more he yelled and cursed at her to move faster and work harder. He would walk behind her and laugh at her pain.

In most cases, he would deny any casual employee's

request for time off. He did have his favorites, usually women who did not reject his sexual advances or complain about his abuse and disrespect. Jen eventually quit because she was in too much pain to come to work one day, and, she knew if she called in sick, she would be fired.

I became popular after the word got around that I was involved in martial arts and I was the author of a book. Soon, guys would talk to me about martial arts and women would talk about my book. The supervisor disapproved of my popularity. It was inconceivable to him that any Black man could be respected unless it was him, a supervisor for the United States Postal Service. To him and the others who profited from getting as much work done by the "casuals" as they could, "casual" was the new name for nigger.

Some career employees had developed a dislike for "casuals" because "casuals" prevented them from getting overtime hours. "Casuals" were forced to work on any and all of the jobs that the career employees did. The career employees could leave after their eight-hour shifts, and if any of their work was left, "casuals" were required to finish the job. We were informed that we could not leave until all of the work was finished. In most cases, we were sent to complete two or three different jobs before we could leave. "Casuals" had to be more qualified than career employees, who were only required to do the job they had been hired to do.

For several months, Mary and I saw each other only in passing because we were on different shifts and had different days off. At the end of our temporary appointments, we were both rehired because we both did our jobs well.

After learning that we were married, a Korean supervisor suggested that we be given the same day off. My supervisor did not approve. It was amusing to him to keep us away from each other. After we were given the same days off, he would usually find some way to switch my day. Neither he or the White supervisor showed any disrespect to Mary; for they did not know how I would react. The White supervisor would often remark that he would not want a man with my skills working for him.

Judy held a job at Baptist Hospital and worked as a casual employee for the United States Postal Service. Judy and I became friends and got close enough to hug whenever we met. My supervisor liked Judy a lot. His attraction for her was obvious. It also became obvious that he did not like me or any other male anywhere near her. The other employees often made jokes about his obsession with keeping us away from each other. On several occasions, loud arguments occurred when some of the career employees started conversations with Judy. The career employees could argue because they had employment rights. "Casuals" could be fired immediately if they talked back. As time passed, Judy began to complain that my supervisor was constantly threatening her to keep other guys away from her.

I did not like the job, but Mary was happy that I was working and I was determined to keep the job at all cost. The supervisor would make jokes about my pain. As he had done with Jen, he made an effort to place me on jobs that he considered hard and when I overheard him telling another employee that he would break me, I was more than ever determined to stick it out. Once again it was like I was in the Marine Corps, being ordered to function while in severe pain. I became determined to keep the job.

Veterans working for the postal service informed me of my ability to take the postal exam for career employment. They told me that, as a career employee, the salary more than doubled, you had benefits, two days off instead of one, eight-hour days instead of twelve and union representation. As a Service-Connected Disabled Veteran, there was no downside to me applying for career employment.

I visited human resources to learn that although no postal exams were being given at the time, by law, a Service-Connected Disabled Veteran could open an exam at any time. The human resources representative, however, had learned about my teaching martial arts and participating in martial arts activities. After finding that I was receiving a disability check, it was decided that I was lying to the government about my disability. The lady was angry that I was doing martial arts and getting a check, and she decided to deny my right to open an exam. I was given a paper advising me of the law, then told the law was no longer in effect.

When one of the supervisors asked Mary and I to bring our tae kwon do uniforms to work so that we could take pictures for the postal a newspaper, I had the feeling that the real reason for the pictures was to prove that I was collecting a disability check illegally.

The longer I worked for the Postal Service, the more I learned about my supervisor and some of the other supervisors. Since the causal positions were held by people who could not find other work and casual employees could be fired at any time, sexual harassment was common. The career employees began to tell stories about numerous cases that had been brought against my supervisor and the way the office covered them up.

He began to hit on Judy. When Judy rejected his advances, he punished her by choosing the hardest jobs for her. I asked her why she did not report him; she said she had a child and needed both jobs. I was pushing a cart of mail one night when I spoke to Judy as I passed. The supervisor threw a tantrum. "Brown!" he yelled. "What in the fuck are you doing, we need the damn mail. Bring the fucking mail on down here. You don't have no fucking time to talk!!"

I wanted to confront him, but I knew I would be fired on the spot, and I could not disappoint my wife. On the other hand, I could not let the matter go because I knew that, once it got stated, the abusive language would only get worse. My pain would cause me to get irritated enough to hit the supervisor and I would end up in jail.

I looked over the papers we had been given when we were hired. The post office's promise that employees would be treated with "dignity and respect" was a joke. When I told some of the other employees that the treatment was actually in writing, signed by the supervisor, they did not believe it.

I wrote to the plant manager about the post office's promise to treat employees with dignity and respect, and about the supervisor's constant yelling and cursing. My complaint was sent to the person who'd been standing right there when the supervisor had done the cursing, and I realized my writing had been in vain.

I was called into this person's office, and told that my supervisor was an Ex-Marine who had been a drill sergeant and that he had brought this drill sergeant mannerisms to the job. I told the gentleman that I had been a Marine also, and any Marine would consider my supervisor a disgrace to the Marine Corps. Drill sergeants used the abusive language when training Marine recruits; they did not continue when the training period was over. In addition, no one in their right mind would want to go on a job where they were treated as if they were going through Marine Corps boot camp.

I became more popular after it was learned that I had reported the supervisor. Some of the career employees told me about his rise to power. I was told that an extreme racist once held the position of supervisor. They said the woman was extremely obese, constantly ate doughnuts, and rarely left her office. When my supervisor was hired, he befriended the woman by belittling Blacks. He would gladly volunteer to do the woman's dirty work when it came time to reprimand or fire Blacks. In return for his service, the woman helped him to get the supervisory position.

The man I'd reported my supervisor to was said to have been hired after him, but was later promoted over him. On several occasions, Whites were promoted to positions that my supervisor felt he should have gotten. He told us that he had been told by a Marine Corps officer that he would always be at a disadvantage because of his skin color. It was obvious that he hated black skin and considered his skin the reason for his problems. Belittling Blacks would prove to the Whites that he was different. Once, when a machine broke down and a White mechanic was sent to repair it, he told the White man, "These machines act just like niggers."

I arrived at work one day to find out that he'd launched a vicious verbal attack on a young lady who worked as a casual employee. He had driven the girl to tears. Everyone's conversation that day was about this shameful, verbal attack on the young lady.

His sexual advances to Judy had also increased. Judy said that her spirit had been broken when, after rejecting one of his advances, she had been ordered to work alone on a machine for twelve hours in an isolated part of the plant for several days. I knew that Alabama was probably the only place these incidents could be allowed to go on without anything being done. I wanted to see what my supervisor would do if he had to face a man without the protection of the United States Postal Service.

I printed up flyers inviting him to fight three rounds as part of a martial arts demonstration. I was careful not to threaten him. I handed a flyer to the White supervisor in order to let him know the offer was for him also. I put some on the bulletin boards and in the break rooms so that everyone in the post office was aware that the challenge had been made.

As the employees learned about the challenge, people began to shake my hand, thanking me for standing up to what they considered to be a monster. When asked if he was going to fight, my supervisor said no and the men and women began to tease him. He even became quiet for nearly a week. Then he began sending me to other supervisors to work. He told them that I was a good worker but he did not like my attitude.

As soon as I began working for the postal service, I informed my supervisor that I needed a few days off in July so that I could visit grand master Cho in Honolulu and test for my second degree Black Belt. My supervisor's response was, "We'll work something out." When the time came, my request was denied.

I had never taken a day off, so I called in sick in order to make the trip. I was so worn out by the six-day, twelve-hour work weeks, I was barely able to perform. I told Mary that I did not feel that I was ready at that time. However, she encouraged me to take the trip anyway. I was in such bad shape when I arrived I put on my worst performance ever. When I told grand master Cho about the job, he did not believe it was possible to make a person work six days a week, twelve hours a day without holidays. "This is the United States," grand master Cho said, "they can't do that." Everyone that I told about the job found it hard to believe.

When the postal exams eventually opened, I took several tests for career positions with the post office. I passed all of the exams. The Black and White supervisors were OK with the way they could keep Mary and I separated with the long hours and six-day schedule. They continued to rehire me for "casual" appointments, however, they were determined that I was not going to get a career position.

There was an opening for the position of "rural carrier." A rural carrier delivered mail from a truck and there was very little walking. The job was perfect for me, and I had passed the exam to qualify me for the position. After I had passed the drug test and all the other requirements for the job, I received a letter to report to a doctor in Georgia for a physical exam. The other veterans wondered why I was sent over three hundred miles for a physical when no one else had been.

The postal service's letter ordered me to report for the physical on June 8, 2004. On June 11, 2004, I reported for work. My supervisor's supervisor instead of George White met me at the time clock and asked me to come to the office, informed me that the orthopedic surgeon who examined me reported that I was unable to stand or walk for over four hours a day.

He said that, because of the doctor's report, I was terminated from the casual position, denied the position of Rural Carrier, and I could not be used on the other positions that I took the tests for. I was asked to turn in my badge and to leave immediately.

I was relieved to leave the post office. I had never

been in a place where there was so much evil. Other veterans told me that it was not right to wait until after I passed the exam to terminate me, and as a service-connected disabled veteran, the law prevented me from being terminated because of my disability.

I filed a discrimination complaint with Equal Employment Opportunity Commission. Although I was not a career employee, the union representative helped me through the process and represented me during the mediation session. During mediation, he asked the higher supervisor why I had not been offered "reasonable accommodations." "Well, Mr. Brown should have asked for reasonable accommodations," came the reply. That was the first time I had heard about reasonable accommodations. Later, lawyers for the postal service would fraudulently report that my case was sent to the reasonable accommodations committee before I was terminated.

After I lost the job, I began to notice changes in Mary that led me to believe she was having an affair and had started using drugs again. She was working six days a week and would disappear on her day off. She began hanging out with a group of young partying people at the post office.

When it was time for us to celebrate thirty years of marriage, Mary and her new friends took a trip to Detroit. I was not invited. Mary's sister had been telling her about the new drug, "Ecstasy." It was some type of pill. I never bothered to learn about the drug. I did ask Mary if she had started getting high again. She said no, but in her eyes I could tell that something was wrong.

After I confronted her about never being at home, Mary moved in with her friends. Once again, I could not blame her for leaving. Our marriage seemed to amount to one hard time after another. Mary continued to work for the postal service as a casual employee. I kept telling her that the twelve-hour, six-day schedule was not healthy, but she seemed to be satisfied with her new life, whatever it was. She was careful not to let me know where she lived, but I was not going to look for her. I just hoped that things were better for her. I assumed that they were, because she would often come by the house to pick up items to be used for parties.

With no job, no wife, and the Department of Education taking part of my disability check, I was behind on the house payment; the water, lights, and gas were shut off, and soon I was almost in the same position I was in when we were in Los Angeles. I was informed that there were laws protecting veterans who lose their job because of service-connected disabilities and advised to report my termination to the Department of Veterans Affairs. The Department of Veterans Affairs simply sent me to another doctor who said that I was OK to work. When I explained to the doctor that I had just been terminated because a doctor said that I could not work, I could see that the doctor found it amusing that I was being denied work because of disability reports from doctors, then denied disability compensation because of doctor reports again I was able to work. Some information about my condition was deliberately omitted by the doctor because it would have helped my case. This was a racist game played by Whites in government positions.

The game had not changed since the Vietnam Era, and it could have been practiced as long as Blacks had been serving in the military. It was hard for me to control my anger. However, I thought about the Black veteran who had gone to prison for bringing a gun into the Veterans Administration Office during the Sixties. I realized that the strategy of White racists was to eliminate legal means of survival and to invest in prisons. The Department of Veterans Affairs had to realize that crime was the only alternative after all legal means of survival had been denied. The criminal justice system was, in reality a means for Whites to live like leeches off minorities.

I began writing the President, Senate, and Congress again, inquiring how they expect service-connected disabled veterans to survive if they are denied work because of disability then denied disability compensation. I asked why was it OK for the government to tell a veteran there is nothing they could do if a veteran had lost his ability to earn a living because he had become disabled while serving the government.

I examined my military records and uncovered some disturbing facts. Falsifying my medical records to prevent me from receiving compensation was only part of the deception. I found that, while serving in the Marine Corps, I had received good grades until the decision was made to discharge me. It was obvious that from that time, my grades took a downward turn to make it look like I was not performing my duties as well as I should have. Then, after forty years, I began to understand the Tijuana jail incident.

While I was waiting to be discharged, I went to Tijuana, Mexico, with two other Marines. We were given overnight passes. However, we were arrested after we got drunk. We notified the Marine Corps that we were locked up in Tijuana, but we never got a reply. The Tijuana jail was like being in another world. The cells were crowded. We were placed in a cell reserved for Americans. There were four beds and twelve people in the cell. The only water available was in a toilet in the center of the cell. If you had money, you could pay the guards for drinking water. The water was delivered in an empty dirty milk carton.

The food consisted of some kind of soup that looked like sewer water because there were fish heads in it with the eyes still in place. At night we were given bread. The bread was all I ate for twelve days.

The guards would take the prisoners' possessions. In one incident, a guard asked one of the Americans if he could see his watch. The guard took the watch and walked off. Some of the Americans would send home for money, the money would be sent, and taken by the guards.

There was a women's cell on the floor below us. At night some of the guards would go into the cells, tape newspaper over the bars, and rape the women. You could hear the screams during the night.

After a few days I decided to break out. When the cell was opened for some of the men to be released, I walked out with the group. I was near the door when they realized I was not due to be released. I threw several guards around and made my way to the street. I got to the border and reported to the Untied States Border Patrol. After a long discussion, the Border Patrol told me that they had to take me back to the jail. They apologized and informed me that they had to maintain a good relations with the Mexican government and they could not aid an escaped prisoner. They did, however, promise to notify the Marine Corps that three Marines were locked up in Tijuana.

After the report from the Border Patrol, Marine Corps officers came to Tijuana to arrange for our release. They asked the Mexican officials not to file charges for my escape. They told me that they knew that I was there, but they decided to leave me in jail for a while in order to teach me a lesson. Looking back, I can see the reason for leaving me in jail was to have me listed as a deserter. If I had not broken out, I would have been charged with desertion. Upon hearing that I had escaped from jail and was returned by my own government, there were some angry Marines.

Although the plan to call me a deserter had failed, the Marine Corps still decided to hold a summary court martial for my being AWOL, in an attempt to place something negative on my record. They would use any means to prevent me from getting disability compensation although I was being discharged for disability. The officer in charge of my court martial was a hard and mean Marine. He was actually proud of my escape from the Tijuana jail. After hearing cases that involved real deserters, he considered my situation a joke. He placed me on probation.

The Marine Corps would still use the incident to place something negative on my record. On my DD Form 214, they underlined "One period lost time on current enlistment." No reason was given for the lost time.

Like the United States Marine Corps, the United States Postal Service would use deception to prevent me from receiving disability compensation. The Department of Veterans Affairs sent forms to the post office inquiring about my termination. Instead of reporting that I was terminated after my physical exam and because of the physical exam, the postal service reported that my employment ended because my appointment had ended. The Department of Veterans Affairs ignored a letter stating I had been terminated because I "failed to meet medical requirements," and used the postal service's falsified report in denying my disability compensation.

Although I was upset about the way my marriage had ended, I understood Mary's feeling that the government would continue to block any means of my being able to support myself or a family. After a few weeks of grief about the loss of my wife, I began to realize that we actually broke up a long time ago, back in Los Angeles. I took it upon myself to find her and rescue her from crack. Maybe she never wanted to be rescued in the first place.

I entered a rehabilitation program with Alabama State rehab. I spent a year going through some computer training and a micro-management program to help me learn about running my own business. I felt uncivilized living without a phone, lights, or gas, but I'd lived through worse. Realizing that the only reason for my problems was the government's refusal to pay disability benefits after I had become disabled while serving in the United States Marine Corps made me continue to write to the President, the Senate, and the Congress for help.

Eventually, the Sheriff came to put me and my property on the streets as they had done years before in Los Angeles. However, this time I did not have to become a gang member to survive. Completion of the rehabilitation program made me eligible to get a grant to open my own business. I lost the house and my belongings, but with help from the grant I was able to rent a place to open my martial arts studio. I spent my days getting my school ready to open, and I slept at my sister's house.

At the age of fifty-eight, I entered the tae kwon do competition at the Alabama State Sports Festival. I won first place and gold medals in sparring, forms, and creative forms. With help from the grant I opened Percy Brown's Institute of Tae Kwon Do in Montgomery, Alabama.

I was getting my school ready to open when Dr. Carlinda Purcell became a member of my church. Dr. Purcell had moved to Alabama to take a position with the school board. After making several positive changes for the school system, Dr. Purcell made headlines when she was abruptly asked to resign her position. The reason given was she would not work with the other board members. The church and the community joined in to support Dr. Purcell. There were mass meetings held in support of Dr. Purcell that reminded me of the meeting Blacks held during the bus boycotts in the sixties after Ms. Rosa Parks refused to give up her seat on the bus.

Dr. Purcell ended up giving up her position, to the disappointment of a lot of Blacks. One man told me that his biggest disappointment was seeing other Blacks helping to bring Dr. Purcell down. Dr. Purcell also talked about her disappointment in the actions of some of the Blacks. My supervisor was not the only Black man determined to help keep his race down. The South was filled with them.

One of Dr. Purcell's supporters quoted her as saying, "The people here are like crabs in a barrel, constantly pulling each other down." In a conversation with my pastor, Reverend Thurman said, "The more thing change, the more they remain the same." He described how bad the situation got during the discussions about Dr. Purcell's job. "Things got really nasty," he told me. It even got to the point where houses were vandalized.

"I guess educators can act like gang members also," I said. "I believe that, especially in the South, people have been subjected to so much evil, their minds have become infected. Too many Blacks have been led to believe that their only means of survival is to help the Whites keep other Blacks down. Life is so miserable for so many Blacks that they become comfortable destroying each other." I paused and thought how some people place Condolezza Rice and Colin Powell in the same category as my supervisor. Gang members even see them as gang members, big-time gang members. "It's a strange world," I said.

When I hear about terrorism, I often wonder if terrorists are people who would rather die than live like some of us have to live. One thing for sure, the statement, "They hate our freedom" is just as misleading as "casual employment."

When I'm alone, I think about Mary and the adventures we shared. I also think about the guys that I shared the most exciting time of my life with. I never saw Kojac again. He ended up on death row; the last thing I heard about him was that he had tried to hang himself twice. I visited Omar after he was released from prison. His hair had grayed a little but he looked well. The last time I saw Blue, he was still surrounded with beautiful girls. I heard that Johnnie-Reb had gotten married, and someone said they had seen Kool in jail.

I heard that Mary had remarried. No matter what happened between us, I sincerely hope that she is happy. I try to think of the good times we shared, but I can't avoid thinking about my last conversation with Omar. His last words to me were, "Twenty-five wherever you go in the world, we will always be brothers, and you can always depend on me to have your back, but I have to be honest with you, I don't trust your wife."

It may be that things would have been different if I had been able to support myself and my family, but as I look back I can't think of anything more valuable than the education I gained from hard times. I don't get hung up on material things—they can be taken too easily. I don't put my faith in humans—they can be disappointing. When I die, I want to go back to the place I visited when I overdosed on drugs. My belief is that a clear conscience is the only way. I have been convinced that every thought and act is rewarded, good or evil.

Acknowledgment

Special thanks to First Lady Rosalyn Carter and Presidents Lyndon B. Johnson, Jimmy Carter, Bill Clinton, and George W. Bush for responding to my letters. Thanks to Ms. Angela Howard.